VIRTUAL FACILITATION & MEETINGS

A Desktop Reference for Running
a Successful Online Classroom

Kevin McAlpin

WORDCATCHERpublishing

Virtual Facilitation and Meetings
A Desktop Reference for Running a Successful Online Classroom

© 2020 Kevin McAlpin
Source images supplied by Adobe Stock
Cover design © David Norrington

Published in the United Kingdom by Wordcatcher Publishing, an imprint of Wordcatcher Publishing Group Ltd
www.wordcatcher.com
Tel: 02921 888321
Facebook.com/WordcatcherPublishing

First Edition: 2020
British Library Cataloguing in Publication Data
A catalogue record for this book is available from the British Library
Print edition ISBN: 9781789423518
Ebook edition ISBN: 9781789423525

Category: Distance Learning / Facilitation

CONTENTS

ACKNOWLEDGEMENTS

This book didn't even exist as an idea at the start of 2020. However, the global COVID-19 pandemic sweeping into our lives changed everything we knew, and everything we did. Business and personal lives were thrown into confusion and, tragically, people passed away.

This book is dedicated to those who continue to work on the front line, keeping us safe and saving lives, and to those working on ways of combatting the virus in the future. We are entering a new world where changes we are experiencing during lockdown and social distancing will undoubtedly persist into the future.

Towards the end of March 2020, as lockdown became likely and then a reality, it became clear that many people would struggle to cope with the isolation and uncertainty. I wanted to do something to help and with a team of over 60 people all volunteering their time, experience, and skills we published *Surviving the Coronavirus Lockdown*: over 50,000 words; involving people from 11 countries; and available free to anyone who wanted it. Through companies sending out the book to employees, and word of mouth it was made available to over one million people within its first month of release. Amazingly, it took less than two weeks from inception to publication.

The book you hold in your hands now is not the book I intended to write in 2020, and neither was *Surviving the Coronavirus Lockdown*. Both were born from the necessity to help people in an uncertain world. This book, too, is a collaboration, with many people to thank for their contributions to its content. In no particular order: David Picton, Edward Gordon-Lennox, Robin Ancrum, Ann Akers, Krushma Makwana, Steve Harvey, Jamie Tott, Beverley McMaster, Mark Edgerton, Carl Rayne, Ali McBride, Andy

Matheson, Cora-Lynn Heimer Rathbone. In particular, my thanks go to Megan Anderson, Steve Apps, Will Carnegie, Matthew Gregory and Ola Lagunju, who generously gave their time and expertise to add to the content of this book.

Thanks to https://rootedinrights.org for accessibility information summarised throughout the book.

Editorially, I am indebted to Michael Millar, Alice McVeigh and David Norrington, for moulding my words, thoughts, and sometimes scruffy notes, into a coherent text. This has been a rushed endeavour, and time has not been on our side. If you spot any typos or inaccuracies, we'd be grateful if you could let us know at admin@wordcatcher.com, so we can rectify them in a future edition. For a future edition is likely as the world changes.

I would also like to thank Wordcatcher Publishing for believing in both *Surviving the Coronavirus Lockdown*, and this book. At a testing time for publishers everywhere, they took both books on with the shared belief that they would be of real value to people at a time when there were so many questions to be answered. I don't know many publishers that could pull this off, not once but twice, in just five months.

Collective experience has made this book better than it would have been had I thought I knew it all and written it alone. This is a theme that runs through this book – you are not alone in facilitating online meetings and classrooms. Help is at hand.

Kevin McAlpin
15th July, 2020

INTRODUCTION

Are you a coach, consultant, teacher, trainer, educator, or learning and development professional?

Are you looking to transfer your knowledge and expertise into the virtual world?

Whether you are new to delivering education online, or an experienced and successful virtual facilitator who wants to hone their skills, this book is for you. Here we share the skills and behaviours of world-class facilitators, focusing on core principles that deliver the best results whatever your goal – be it facilitation, training, teaching or running meetings.

This is a guide for coaches, consultants, teachers, trainers, educators and learning and development professionals.

Deliver industry-leading live virtual learning sessions using effective strategies and you will engage your participants to get the results you, and they, need.

Facilitating learning in online classrooms is going to increase, not only while COVID-19 restricts our ability to get together, but well into the future. Companies will no doubt review their travel, accommodation and training budgets, and online learning is well placed to deliver significant cost savings. But will there be a cost in terms of quality? It will be the job of innovative educators to ensure that quality learning isn't sacrificed for convenience, and the outcomes of online learning reaps rewards for all involved – and, principally, for the learner.

The global pandemic has changed the way the world does business, perhaps forever. Many activities that were carried out face-to-face as a matter of course are now being done in the virtual world, equally matter-of-factly. We estimate that up to half of face-to-face facilitation will be replaced by virtual delivery when the 'new normal' embeds itself in our professional lives.

This new world requires significant new skills, and not least in the realms of learning and development. It offers new challenges to overcome, but big opportunities for those that can thrive in it.

We have designed this book to deliver what you need succinctly and in immediately actionable ways. You will learn how to:

- Transfer skills learned in the face-to-face world into the virtual environment.
- Master virtual facilitation, from preparation to delivery.
- Use interactive and participative tools to deliver creative sessions.
- Energise and engage your participants to bring out the best in them.
- Transfer your learning and development programmes to virtual delivery.

The types of events this will help you to manage include:

- virtual classrooms
- team-building events
- in-house training
- leadership and talent development
- meetings
- conferences

This book assumes that readers are already experienced and qualified to deliver facilitation and learning. It is not our job to teach educators how to educate, facilitators to facilitate, or presenters to present. What we will highlight, however, is how virtual is different to face-to-face, and how a blended approach can work. Some suggestions may seem obvious, particularly to those with decades of experience, but we don't want to miss out some of the simple points that can otherwise be overlooked.

CONTRIBUTORS

The strategies and tactics in this book will work whatever stage of the journey you are on. It is the product of six expert facilitators' years of experience. These are the strategies that have worked for us across the globe and now they can work for you. We have worked for some of the world's leading brands and organisations. From Europe, Africa, Asia, the Middle East, North and South America, and Oceania, we have transformed virtual classrooms, directed remote team meetings, led conferences and injected major companies with new enthusiasm for live online learning.

Here's that experience in numbers:

- 700+ educators taught to present, design and deliver virtually
- 1,000+ virtual meetings facilitated
- 6,000+ virtual sessions delivered
- 12,000+ hours of virtual delivery
- ...all delivered on multiple platforms
- ...collectively delivered with over half of the UK's FTSE 100 companies

You're in safe hands – we can help you to scale up and refine your delivery.

KEVIN MCALPIN

Kevin is managing director of Performance Coaching International and one of the UK's leading executive and team performance coaches. A leadership development specialist, he delivers one-on-one and group sessions both face-to-face and virtually to senior executives from major companies and governments across the globe, including 47 out of 100 of the current FTSE companies.

Kevin regularly speaks at conferences and appears in the media as a pioneering leader in developing new ways of leadership and learning, focused on his specialist areas of organisational learning, building trust and reputation, and having courageous conversations.

Kevin has worked closely with the following contributors to put this book together, drawing on a team, just as he does when facilitating sessions.

MEGAN ANDERSON

For over twenty years, Megan has designed and facilitated solutions to enhance leadership, team and organisational performance, in a broad range of industries.

For the past ten years she has focused on helping to become fluent in the virtual working environment. She has worked with over 1,000 members of diverse teams and cultures in over twenty countries addressing the many challenges of cross-cultural teamworking and changes in working practices due to the digital shift.

STEVE APPS

Steve specialises in helping leaders to be better communicators. He has a technical background, having started out as a computer software trainer, which helped with the move from facilitating face-to-face to virtual delivery.

He ran his first virtual classroom in 2012 and has since run close to 100 virtual coaching and training sessions with groups from 2–200. Given that leaders often have to communicate virtually, this has become an area of specialism for Steve.

How do you pitch for business when your client is on the other side of the world? How do you pitch ideas to people to gain traction and commitment? How do you ensure you maximise your leadership impact when presenting and influencing virtually? These are questions to which Steve helps leaders find answers. He adopts an evidence-based approach, ensuring that his work is grounded in well-established theory and the latest research.

WILL CARNEGIE

Will has been consulting and coaching in physical and virtual settings since 2001 and uses a range of experiences from the worlds of sport, the military, risk industries (including energy and shipping) and business, to inform his approach.

His passion for developing people stems from his experiences gained leading a team of seventeen crew members around the world in the BT Global Challenge sailing race in 2000/01.

He completed the Institute of Leadership and Management (ILM) Level 7 in Executive Coaching course in 2018 and is one of only a handful of UK coaches accredited to use the Executive Arts resources. He also coaches young people in sailing as a qualified Royal Yachting Association (RYA) Instructor.

MATTHEW GREGORY

Matthew has been working in the field of personal and organisation change for the thick end of thirty years. Before starting his own business in 2007, he spent nine years working as a senior manager at KPMG.

He has designed and led countless leadership and personal skills programmes, ranging from one-hour to twelve-month transformation programmes. He has worked extensively in both the face-to-face and virtual classroom environments. He also co-designed a programme that helped experienced in-person facilitators to excel in delivering courses in a virtual classroom: over 300 people have so far graduated from it.

OLA LAGUNJU

Ola is an experienced organisational development and inclusion consultant, with over twenty years international business experience gained both as a consultant and internal practitioner. A significant part of her career has been spent working in the retail industry where posts held included Head of Learning, and Executive Development.

Her last corporate role was Head of Organisation Development for one of Europe's largest retailers, where she was responsible for delivering large-scale transition and organisational renewal projects, and helped to establish a culture of inclusion and engagement after a major organisational restructure.

Her emphasis throughout her career has been on creating virtual and live programmes that leverage difference.

THRIVING
IN THE VIRTUAL WORLD

THE CHANGED CONTEXT

The sudden boom in virtual facilitation has been driven by very particular and peculiar circumstances. But that doesn't mean it's *all* going to go away any time soon... if ever. The global crisis caused by the COVID-19 pandemic has turned virtual learning from a steady and growing trend into a stampede.

It has triggered a sharp spike in the use of live virtual events and, at the same time, brought about a dramatic change in behaviour across the world. Virtual learning and working have been embraced and have become the norm where they weren't before. Even the most cynical have been forced to accept the benefits for employees, businesses and the planet, through reduced costs, time, environmental impact, and so on.

More importantly, they've realised that when it's done well it *works*. This fits with the trend towards flexible and remote working that has been growing for some time and, in turn, can boost a company's brand, recruitment and retention, and productivity.

Those who do not understand the online world and cannot work with it will likely be left behind. This is a serious issue for many facilitators and mistakes and missed opportunities lie in wait for the unprepared and unwary.

DON'T GET LEFT BEHIND

It was a challenging transition for someone who was getting sizzling reviews and face-to-face ratings to suddenly switch to online – to face horrible critiques and ratings of 3/10! As a colleague described gloomily: 'Listen, I'm trying to engage these people and I just can't get the same response. It's like I've just had all my limbs cut off. I'm just staring at the blinking webcam, wondering what I can do!'

It doesn't have to be this way. In fact, if you follow our advice, you can learn to relish the chance to use virtual facilitation as part of a blended approach – as we have done with some of the world's largest organisations.

To aid this transition, we've focused on the key aspects of virtual facilitation that you need to understand in this brave new world. These factors will give you an in-depth understanding of the environment you are now operating in.

HORSES FOR COURSES

There are aspects you may find easy and some you might find more difficult – and they differ from person to person. For example, there are some people who appear less charismatic in a crowded room and find virtual facilitation a *more* comfortable environment in which they can thrive. Others who excel face-to-face might find the change in proximity, energy and technology far more daunting.

Most of us learn through trial and error, but our hope is that you learn from our experience of what works – and avoid the scars of what went wrong. Whatever your challenges, we will help to dramatically speed up your personal journey to mastery.

DOES VIRTUAL LEARNING WORK?

You might welcome virtual learning with open arms, or it might feel as though it is something that has been forced on you by the sudden changes brought on by the pandemic. There are plenty who disparage its impact and effectiveness but, like it or loathe it, virtual learning, blended learning and face-to-face learning have *equal* impact on behavioural change and skill development.

Virtual learning is not in competition with, or a replacement for, face-to-face. It can be a substitute and can also work brilliantly within a blended approach – combining elements of face-to-face, virtual and self-directed learning.

This is fortunate because, as we previously mentioned, our estimate is that up to half of face-to-face learning will disappear forever to be replaced by online options. That's a staggering change for educators to adapt to.

The future is all about blended learning. When you think about it, this is unsurprising. Learning is a cognitive, social and emotional experience that can be delivered both physically and virtually. And, in some ways, it's been slow in coming. Facebook didn't stop social gatherings and YouTube didn't stop concerts. TV didn't kill reading, and ebooks didn't stop people reading paperbacks. What they did do was change the balance of how consumers behave and this is exactly what is happening in the learning realm now. What we are left with is the question of why is face-to-face needed? Can it be justified? The old assumption that it's the only way to educate is now in question.

Live, virtual training is only a part of the equation, and a cleverly blended approach is often the best option. There are a lot of factors that determine what a cleverly blended approach looks like in any given environment, including: the outcome you are looking to achieve; time available to plan and deliver; budget; organisational culture; and the learning styles of the participants.

You may be surprised to know it may not be the *method* of delivery that makes the difference: instead, it's the *design* of the learning process and the conscious determination to achieve the desired improvement in mindset, behaviour or skill.

It's as possible in the virtual world as in the real world to give people an experience of something stretching, something that takes them outside their comfort zone and primes them for learning, adjustments and change. This is essential if you want to support people to be emotionally component, resilient and able to deal with the situations people typically encounter.

Ashridge Management College looked at the different modes of blended learning to see which one was the most effective in changing behaviour and developing skills. They took three different scenarios: 1) in-person, face-to-face; 2) a combined approach of virtual, self-direction and face-to-face learning; and 3) entirely virtual. They used a rigorous methodology for measuring impact, not only in respect of stress levels – via heart-rate monitors – but also in follow-up research, in terms of impact on both learned behaviours and skills.

They found each of these three methods were *equally* effective at delivering changes in behaviour and developing skills. The study concluded that the following factors seemed to have the greatest impact on participants:

- Whether there was an emotional experience where they encountered an intense learning point, one outside their normal, day-to-day experience, which they often struggled to make sense of initially.
- Whether they were supported to make sense of this learning point, to reflect and to analyse it with someone – a peer, a colleague or a coach. This

enabled them to consciously understand and plan how to put their insight into practice.

- Whether the subsequent development plan was implemented using mutual support, encouragement, positive feedback and accountability. This included fostering a feeling that 'We're all in this together, with people we trust', and whether they had a plan to transfer that key learning moment into action.

THE WIDER CASE FOR VIRTUAL LEARNING

Academic research shows a strong case for virtual learning, in terms of the benefits it brings to participants. But is it also important to understand the wider practical case for virtual learning if we are to appreciate the impact it can have on facilitators (and their businesses), event participants, firms and society more widely.

These results not only support the case for virtual learning, but help promote *even more* of it. They include:

THE BUSINESS CASE

Virtual learning is good for business and also morally justifiable. The benefits for people, profit and the planet include: reduced costs, time savings, and lower carbon emissions due to reduced travel. All of which further enables companies to align themselves with the trends for flexible and remote working.

INCLUSIVITY

People living in different time zones to the organisers, or with other challenges such as childcare, can still attend courses. Furthermore, people with the kind of disabilities that make travelling challenging can attend meetings and conferences that would otherwise have been entirely inaccessible to them. In this way virtual learning can broaden the reach of an event and the number of participants. For international organisations, virtual engagement can break down longstanding societal barriers and create a stronger sense of a global community.

DEEPENING THE KNOWLEDGE POOL

This may seem obvious, but you could arrange to have five experts from Sri Lanka, Germany, South Africa, the USA and Chile and they can all share and learn without even leaving their office, whereas even the most committed organisations might struggle to get them to the same conference.

DIVERSITY

Insights can be driven by different cultures and levels of the organisation. Conversations can be held across the globe: a CEO in India, the head of operations in UK or a guest speaker from Brazil can speak with frontline operatives in the Philippines, Canada and Angola. The diversity as well as the number of people one can engage is dramatically increased.

GREATER LEVELS OF ENGAGEMENT

For participants where English is their second language, you can often get stronger engagement, as they feel less intimidated and they can choose to either write (type) or speak.

FLEXIBILITY

Virtual learning can be delivered at the point of need, as people can be sitting in their home or office, taking less time away from work. Peer-to-peer engagement, post-event, is also simpler.

COMMUNITY

Many people are already comfortable in the virtual space: for example, those who have grown up with live gaming platforms. They genuinely feel a part of the online world because they're accustomed to combining gaming with socialising and learning. Similarly, there are those across all ages who feel more open and comfortable in their own personal space and find it easier to engage while at home.

IMPACT

You can make that emotional and personal connection with people virtually and you can do emotionally sensitive work – assuming you create a safe emotional space for people. This has always been part of our job as facilitators and remains unchanged.

REFLECTION TIME

You can record the session and extend the experience, to some degree, for those who missed it live. Participants who made the class can also take advantage of this, choosing to replay the event for reinforcement or reflection.

CONVENIENCE

It can be great for leaders and facilitators to be caught up in the whirl of business travel. However, there's also something wonderful about ending the work day comfortably curled up in your own home. Not to mention reducing the drain travel can make on your creative energy and bottom line.

THE TOP 5 PRIORITIES OF VIRTUAL FACILITATION

Let's start with our priorities as a virtual facilitator, educator or leader. Yes, our role may essentially be the same virtually as it is face-to-face, but the context has changed and so, therefore, must our priorities. We need to adapt.

There are five significant areas requiring attention in the transition from face-to-face to virtual. You must prioritise, be ruthless, and have a laser focus in these five areas.

1. BUILD A SAFE ENVIRONMENT

Your primary purpose is to create an atmosphere and safe environment for learning and decision-making where people want to join in – and want to stay. Setting the right tone for the session will ensure participants stay engaged. Get this wrong and everything that follows becomes much more difficult, or impossible.

2. GUIDE THE CONVERSATION

Your job is to guide conversations and build the relationships with the goal of harnessing the collective energy to a common purpose: developing skills, knowledge and behaviours to maximise the experience. Presenters aren't the focus of attention in the same way as in face-to-face delivery.

3. CREATE AN INTERACTIVE EXPERIENCE

Your creative design must ensure that participants are completely present: doing, responding, talking and being involved – *not* merely passively listening. Distraction sets in quickly online – so maintaining engagement is a constant focus.

4. TAKE CHARGE

You are the director of time and process, taking people skilfully and intuitively through from start to finish. People's expectations are that technology runs smoothly in the background so practise, practise, practise. You must be clear and explicit and signpost participants throughout the session in a way that differs from the real world.

5. USE YOUR SKILLS

Your in-depth knowledge remains the foundation of your content. Your goal is to challenge, support, share and inspire. This should be familiar ground for experienced facilitators. It's delivery that needs to change, not the underlying knowledge to be imparted.

10 MYTHS ABOUT VIRTUAL LEARNING

There are some myths and misconceptions about virtual learning that many of us started with – and which we regularly face with clients and learners. Many of these roadblocks won't go away until openly challenged, so let us help you with that conversation.

MYTH #1:

'Virtual facilitation is just while COVID is around and everything will revert back to face-to-face and normal.'

THE TRUTH:

Our estimate is that up to half of face-to-face training will disappear. Virtual is here to stay; we need to get used to it.

MYTH #2:

'You can't do meaningful work in the virtual space: you can't engage people in the same way. It's just not as effective: you can't do the same things as in a physical experience – you just can't change mindsets and behaviours in the same way.'

THE TRUTH:

If you set the right design environment people will do meaningful work and they will change behaviour. The right facilitator can do great work in a virtual space.

MYTH #3:

'Online is OK, but it's a download of information. People just shove a load of content into sessions and cram it all in. The participants just have a ton of information coming at them down a one-way street.'

THE TRUTH:

Again, this comes down to design. Yes, you absolutely can offer a pre-recorded webinar, but that is entirely different to a live interactive session where people are engaged throughout. 'Interactive' means engaging people as often as every two or three minutes.

MYTH #4:

'If someone's a brilliant face-to-face facilitator they're sure to be brilliant online. It's simple: you just turn your camera on – just a different method of delivery. You don't really have to change anything; what worked in the room will work exactly the same online: no worries!'

THE TRUTH:

You must adapt your style to be successful. From the technological requirements to personal style, this requires time, effort and practice.

MYTH #5:

'I'm intuitive – I know how to 'read' a room – and I can do just the same virtually, so I really don't need to follow process or stick to schedules. Flexibility is key: I can just switch a few things and, believe me, people don't even notice!'

THE TRUTH:

If you do this, at best, you will overrun, miss your objectives and annoy everyone. Virtual sessions require a lot more design.

MYTH #6:

'I'm not a technology expert – I don't have the time to be a tech expert, and, besides, live online classrooms aren't what corporations want.'

THE TRUTH:

This is simply not an option. Technology is here to stay. You are heading for dinosaur status if you don't evolve.

MYTH #7:

'For me, virtual is second class, a last resort. I'd only use this medium when there's nothing else. I can't see any advantage to it; it's passive.'

THE TRUTH:

This isn't true. Practical experience and academic research both show it delivers the same outcomes as face-to-face *if* it is tailored appropriately.

MYTH #8:

'You can't have a courageous conversation online: you'll just have to wait for an in-person meeting. You know the kind of thing: "You missed the deadline on Project Aristotle" or "You didn't speak in Tuesday's virtual meeting and your webcam was off."'

THE TRUTH:

Yes, you can. If you are prepared the environment, and you have your examples and evidence, you are able to accomplish this.

MYTH #9:

'There isn't the same level of accountability in online meetings. If you don't show up nobody will notice.'

THE TRUTH:

If you've agreed with individuals the importance of turning up and they've said they will turn up, the same level of accountability applies.

11 DIFFERENCES BETWEEN VIRTUAL & FACE-TO-FACE DELIVERY

Here are the top eleven differences between virtual and face-to-face facilitation. We will explore each in greater detail throughout this book.

1. DIAL UP WARMTH, EMPATHY AND HUMANITY

You will also need to share your real self earlier than you would in the physical world to help overcome what can be a more sterile virtual environment. The first ten minutes of any virtual meeting or classroom is critical. Allowing participants to practise with the technology really helps. It will set the atmosphere and tone of the whole session.

2. CREATE A TRUSTING ENVIRONMENT, QUICKLY

You'll need to be more deliberate in creating an environment where people are willing to be open. In a virtual environment it takes longer for people to trust you and others in the meeting, and to understand whether it is OK to say what they really think or whether they are simply expected to just tow the party line.

3. TALK LESS

The leadership dynamic is different. You must talk less. With your instructions and questions, you need to be much clearer and completely explicit. More of the learning comes from the conversations between participants and less from you. Your job is to make those conversations happen and manage them.

4. SET GROUND RULES

Agreeing ground rules and etiquette are important, so things run smoothly, distractions are avoided, people are clear that their opinion is valued (even if they're disagreeing with everyone else) and they're clear you want their active participation.

5. MAINTAIN CONTROL

Your style needs to be more direct and – if you're naturally collaborative – this can feel uncomfortable at first. However, if you don't maintain control, conversations can easily get messy, with everyone attempting to talk at once (although this is less likely with agreed ground rules in place). In the physical world you have more time to go off-piste and then return to the topic. Online doesn't afford you this luxury.

6. DESIGN, DESIGN, DESIGN

Your session needs to be designed more closely in terms of detail, structure and timing. It will take longer to produce and you will need to take out around 80% of your content.

7. MAKE THE CAMERA WORK FOR YOU

You are acting like a film crew now. Your camera is for making eye contact with participants on your behalf. You must also take time and be deliberate about your backdrop, camera angle, lighting, sound and what people can see.

8. RECOGNISE THE TIME-WARP EFFECT

There is a time warp: twenty seconds online feels like minutes offline – silences seem to last an age and you have to get used to it. Open questions to the group like, 'How are we feeling?' usually get no reply, and a tumbleweed moment.

9. PREPARE FOR TECHNOLOGY FAILURES

You must be prepared and know what you will say when the technology goes wrong – as it inevitably will. Much more on this to follow.

10. MAINTAIN ACTIVITY

You need to work harder and keep participants busier than you would in a face-to-face environment. If they are passive listeners then they quickly become distracted and may end up checking emails, doing other work, and so on. Make sure you regularly engage with them, maybe with a poll, breakout room, in-chat questions and commentary. People need to be doing something within the first few minutes otherwise they are likely to disengage. In a similar vein, encouraging people to put their webcam on is vital as it's easy to for them feel anonymous or actively disengage, and likewise other participants find it harder to engage with them.

11. BE EXPLICIT

You must talk through what you are doing in a more explicit fashion than you might be used to, so people understand exactly what is happening. For example, if you are going to play a video, then say: 'I am going to share a video,' otherwise they hear silence and this causes confusion. This signposting is crucial whenever you are moving onto another subject, point, question or whatever. It might feel strange at first, but it makes your event feel natural and clearer.

SIMILARITIES OF VIRTUAL & FACE-TO-FACE DELIVERY

We've touched on differences between virtual and face-to-face, particularly in how you deliver it, but many of the foundational principles remain the same, regardless of the delivery method.

The key skills and principles that made you an effective facilitator in the physical world transfer directly to face-to face. And why shouldn't this be the case? After all, with small modifications, people are having parties online, as well as fitness and dance classes, music lessons, counselling, church services and much more besides.

The success of every type of meeting still depends on:

- your level of skill as a facilitator
- the quality of your preparation
- your relationship with participants
- your understanding of their needs and wants.
  Remember: it's still all about *them!*

You can work effectively with participants on almost all skills in a virtual environment – from giving and receiving feedback, coaching, having courageous or sensitive conversations, improving presentational skills or empowering trust, empathy and creativity. *Experiential learning* (learning through experience by first doing an activity and then reflecting on the experience) can be done in exactly the same way virtually as face-to-face.

Meeting physically *before* working together virtually helps – but isn't compulsory. Similarly, people often say, 'Let's leave this until we properly see each other!' but this view deserves to be challenged. It's probably true that in-person is best for courageous conversations, but virtually live is certainly next best (as a last resort on the phone – never by text or social media). You might have to wait 3–6 months to see someone face-to-face, and some issues won't wait that long.

Facilitators have a great opportunity to speed up some of these processes, potentially enabling quicker decisions and helping participants make or save money. It is up to facilitators to set a safe environment for people to have virtual courageous conversations. We will go into more depth on how to create such an environment shortly.

Interestingly, many people feel the complete opposite: they feel *more* comfortable in the virtual world. They feel it flattens social and work hierarchies and allows them to feel less intimated. As a result, they will challenge more, have difficult conversations and make more courageous decisions when their leader is not in the same room but on a screen. For some introverts this also increases their likelihood of speaking up.

SKILLS FOR
THE VIRTUAL EDUCATOR

AUTHENTICITY – BEING REAL IN A VIRTUAL WORLD

As facilitators in virtual meetings, classrooms and learning sessions, we must accept that we will be required to be human and vulnerable. It is an environment where we have to be true to ourselves; one where we 'bring our whole selves' to work and share personal information. Perhaps this was always an inevitable development of the changed world: people can now see the books on your shelves, your cat slinking across camera, the knick-knacks on your desk. To be effective, you have to actively and deliberately set out your personal stall in a quicker and more comprehensive way than you would in a physical environment.

As part of your preparation you need to decide what you want to share about yourself and what's going on in your life in a deliberate fashion. You need to do this in terms what's happening for your participants and how that relates to what's happening to you. To get this right:

- Put yourself in their shoes – what might they be experiencing?
- Consider what impact those experiences might be having.
- Work out what you are willing to share in that context.

We understand this may seem strange. You are introducing a level of familiarity right from the start that wouldn't be normal in a physical environment. But if you don't do this you won't create an environment of honesty and trust that is conducive to learning and growing.

At the same time, you need to be honest with how what you reveal and how you present yourself. We've all seen interviewees on TV who have organised their bookshelf to show you their most intellectual tomes. If you are a literary professor then this might be an appropriate backdrop (and probably close to reality) but if it doesn't reflect who you are and what you do, it can make it harder to connect with people. They usually see through affectations and will wonder who the real you is. Make sure your environment represents the real you.

Moreover, it's tough trying to be someone you're not. The anxiety this instils drains energy and dulls focus, generally leading to less satisfactory outcomes. By contrast, the transition to authenticity requires high levels of trust through open and honest encounters – which can feel liberating.

The traditional maxim still stands: being authentic allows us to connect with people more easily, which makes it easier for everyone to perform at their best. Technology has simply amplified the need to do more of this sharing early on. Once you embrace this, it makes facilitating a whole lot easier.

People tend to think that online learning is detached and results in less of a community feeling when you take part in it. But the remote aspects of virtual events don't mean they have to feel remote. By boosting the warmth, empathy and openness you normally bring to physical sessions, people will feel they have something in common with you and, from the start, you can begin building good relationships.

Finally, it's really important to remember that the participants are on our 'side'. They want this to go well and they also understand that life, and internet connections, are imperfect. If you are honest, open, calm and flexible, they'll look to support you, even when the equipment lets you down with an audible thud. And the best way to prepare for being honest, open, calm and flexible is to:

- Acknowledge this *will* happen.
- Work out what could go wrong in advance.
- Work out what you'll say when it *does* go wrong.

When you move into virtual facilitation there's bound to be a little uncertainty – just as when you first started facilitating face-to-face. But you'll get there and, with a bit of practice, you'll enjoy it immensely.

SELF-EVALUATION & PRACTICE

Record your early sessions and play them back so that you can learn what you need to work on most – however painful this might feel. This is hard to do and may seem like a waste of time. Few people relish the sound of their own voice, or love the way they look on screen.

However, you'll learn more from watching your past performances than almost any other form of feedback. When you can see it and hear it for yourself the evidence is clear. It contributes disproportionately positively to your continued development and will accelerate your expertise. We strongly recommend you do not ignore evaluating your past work.

Things you should be looking out for include:

- mannerisms
- patterns of speech
- pacing of the event
- eye contact you made with the camera, rather than points around your screen
- how naturally you move
- which voice levels you chose

You'll also notice (more judgmentally than any other person) ums, wells, and you know what I means. The truth is in face-to-face interactions these filler words don't register, but in the magnified environment of the virtual world, they can become more noticeable and even annoying. If you're committed to being a strong online communicator, you have to go through the process of taking your performance apart and practising.

It takes practice, practice and then more practice. *If* you do that you will find you know your content and delivery inside out, ensured the ums and ahs are minimised and are happy with the speed and tone of delivery (including deliberate pauses).

Helpful activities to reduce filler words include:

- relaxing – people use more fillers when they're nervous
- catch yourself doing it – watching your performances back is very helpful
- preparation – the best speakers rehearse and know exactly what they're going to say, so filler words tend to disappear
- never read off a list of bullet points
- tell stories rather than reading off sides

BODY LANGUAGE

Facial expressions are not the only non-verbal signals we can convey to participants. You can use your hands and voice to support your questions or key points and to enhance your virtual presence.

People often imagine that the only non-verbal communication cues we have to work with online are facial expressions, but it isn't that simple. For example, if you stand or if you sit up and position the screen correctly people can easily see your hands – and these can be more expressive than you might think! We will look at a number of hand gestures that can help, or hinder, your communication.

THE WAY IT IS

Extending your hands, palms down, offers the unspoken message: 'Listen up, people, this is true.' It's assertive without being aggressive and is a powerful way to help drive home a point, almost a statement in itself. You may use one hand or both.

THE QUESTIONER

This move is done with palms up and moving slightly upwards. It conveys the message 'Look, I'm being open with you,' and also works when asking a question of participants, as an invitation.

THE THINKER

Chin resting in hand with head slightly tilted as you listen. Avoid touching the mouth – this can indicate that you're holding back a comment or disbelief in what's being heard. This gesture helps you let participants know that you are considering what is being said and can also buy you time when you're reaching for the answer to a question.

THE POINTER

You point above the screen and above participants' heads and repeat the phrase or key point. This provides emphasis verbally and non-verbally, powerfully and subliminally, the key message. It literally drives the point home. Be careful of overuse, as it can be perceived as exaggerated or aggressive. You might choose to use this gesture only once in the presentation to really make your main point.

HANDS UP!

When things go wrong, it's is a good idea to literally put your hands up, in order to acknowledge that things have not gone to plan. Even if it's the internet connection or the action of a colleague or participant – and nothing to do with you – this makes people feel better.

EYE CONTACT

Eye contact is a different ballgame in the virtual world. We're not talking about you looking into the eyes of each participant, but looking at the camera or little green dot. This might feel unnatural, but it is really important. No doubt you have been involved in virtual meetings, so you'll already know how easy it is for participants to feel anonymous. Eye contact with the camera will make participants feel you engaging with them personally.

Remembering to do this can take time to embed. Do whatever you need to do to remind yourself to look at the camera.

Put a note with a smiley face or an arrow pointing to your camera to remind you to give eye contact.

Don't worry that you aren't constantly looking directly at their faces or picking up all their facial cues because there are other indicators to look out for, including: who is (or isn't) asking questions; who is involved in the chat; who is taking part in polls; etc.

HOW YOU SOUND

Your voice has a critical importance in the virtual world. You need to consider:

- pitch
- volume
- speed
- energy level

PITCH

This is the musical quality of one's voice. Also called cadence, this is the way your voice rises and falls across a sentence or phrase. There are a number of common variations in pitch but these are most noticeable at the end of a sentence. For example, going up in pitch implies a question and injects a note of uncertainty – it can elicit a response from the listener, too. Going down at the end of a phrase is commanding and implies inner confidence.

Some presenters hardly vary their pitch at all. The monotone effect implies (perhaps unfairly) a lack of interest or enthusiasm.

VOLUME

The ideal volume in an online facilitation is frankly somewhere between medium and strong. Any louder and you run the risk of sounding aggressive, but any softer and you're certain to communicate a lack of confidence – if people can hear you properly at all.

To get this right try recording yourself. This will also ensure you know your correct microphone level settings.

Another option is get advice from your colleagues or clients, ideally over the platform you are going to use.

Be sure you check at the start of every session: 'Can everyone hear me OK?' and if the reply is 'No' that you know how to change your levels.

SPEED

Online, people tend to speed up their words-per-minute speech rate. This can sound as if they're either nervous or impatient (or both) and is usually a function of not being accustomed to the environment.

As a general rule, you should try to speak slightly slower than your normal talking speed and to add very short pauses frequently to allow people to absorb what you've said. This gives participants time to breathe, too.

VOCAL ENERGY

This is the amount of oomph in your voice, and contributes to the feeling of interest, sincerity and enthusiasm. You need more of this than you might think.

If you do TV or radio broadcast training, for example, you will be advised to add extra energy and ask someone to evaluate whether you sound more enthusiastic as opposed to manic. Cameras have the effect of zapping your energy, so you need to be consciously more energetic. The same is true of the virtual learning world.

This energy comes from your breathing. If you breathe from the top of your chest (shallow breathing) you won't have enough energy in your voice. Try using your stomach muscles when you breathe and notice the difference – energy will naturally fall and rise. At the start of a new sentence, or change in subject, it'll feel easier to inject warmth and energy.

BODILY FUNCTIONS

If you are talking and you know you are going to sneeze or cough – or you know there is going to be some other background noise – the best thing is to temporarily put yourself onto mute. It doesn't sound good. Better to go silent for a moment than cause a violent interruption!

MAINTAINING YOUR ENERGY

Virtual facilitation is often more physically and mentally demanding than delivering face-to-face sessions. You need to prepare yourself between sessions to maintain your energy levels, not just for your voice.

There are some very simple reasons why this will be so. Although it might feel strange because you haven't been anywhere, this is actually one of the factors. Because you are less physically mobile, and physicality feeds energy, you are lacking some of the movement you would normally get when training face-to-face.

Humans aren't designed to sit down for long periods (although we do) and it's highly unlikely that you'd normally deliver face-to-face sitting down for the whole presentation, unless you have to.

Also, you're focusing on a far, far smaller working space *and* multi-tasking *and* trying to consciously read people's verbal and non-verbal cues from a screen – all at once.

In large groups you need to get used to saying something and getting no reaction, since you're likely to have put them all on mute. At first, this can be horribly off-putting and energy draining; we're so used to seeing people's reactions, the nods, the smiles, the little grunts of agreement and engagement. Suddenly, *that's all disappeared!* Instead, you're going to have to trust that people can hear you, trust that they're engaged and trust that your design is working. At the same time you need to be wary of silence. If you aren't getting the reactions you expect, it could be because the participants are doing too much listening. Remember, you need to keep this interactive and have them doing something active every two to three minutes if you can.

So, consider how many sessions you are willing/able to run in one day and whether you can present at a high level during back-to-back sessions. Start small and build up, not the other way around.

Some simple ways of keeping your energy up include:

- taking breaks
- staying active during breaks
- going outside or at least moving around
- switching off your phone to limit distractions
- using humour to lift the mood of your participants and yourself
- having snacks and drinks handy if you need to keep physical energy up, or your throat lubricated – but don't slurp or consume it when talking

There are some important new habits you'll want to create, so this becomes second-nature when facilitating online. You may not be aware of them, but you have a set of habits that influence the way you educate face-to-face.

PACE YOURSELF

Create a personal limit of how many sessions you're willing to run in a day and stick to it. As a rule of thumb: two virtual classrooms in a day is magic, with three as the maximum. After you've delivered four sessions in a day you'll probably regret it.

TAKE BREAKS (NOT JUST IN-SESSION)

Breaks are generally good energy boosts for you as well as for attendees. Take a break yourself when you let everyone else have one in the session. It can feel hugely tempting to do emails in breaks but a walk is better.

And take breaks between sessions. It's just as important to re-charge between sessions as it is in them. Scheduling breaks doesn't mean a break from a session to do *different* work – it means a break from *all* work.

CUT OUT DISTRACTIONS

While delivering, have your phone switched off, otherwise it can be tempting take a sneaky peek at your texts or social media. The same goes for email (unless it's necessary to your presentation). You will have enough going on without further distractions, any of which are energy drainers. Close all applications and browser windows that aren't essential to your presentation.

KEEP CUTTING

Once you've mastered your content and technology, try to use fewer (but punchier) slides as this will help to maintain energy by limiting the different elements in play during a session.

MUSIC

Using music can also lift your spirits, in breaks and during reflective sessions for delegates. Give participants the choice to listen to it or not as they wish. Enjoy a multi-sensory experience.

THE BEST HABIT IS TO DEVELOP GOOD HABITS

The effort you put in outside sessions will be of greatest help. Do whatever you can to be in a good place physically and mentally. Meditation, mindfulness, tennis, jogging... whatever works for you. Routines really help. Have a routine and stick to it.

FOOD & DRINK

Ensure you have sufficient food and drink for your session to keep you hydrated and energised.

THIS IS FUN

Some of the best learning comes when we're having fun. And some of the best teaching, too. So, whenever you can, smile! It's infectious. Happiness leads us to smile, and people will imitate your mood – positive or negative. Smiling, regardless of how you feel, will make you happier. So, smile and the world does indeed smile with you. Don't forget to have some fun – it's good for you, and it's good for your participants.

DEALING WITH DIFFICULT SITUATIONS

You must know how to act when faced with a participant who is either uninvolved in your session, interrupting or not taking your presentation seriously.

How do you have a conversation with the only person who isn't seriously participating? That one person who doesn't even trouble to mute themselves so everyone can hear them cracking jokes? Or, perhaps someone is upset and doesn't want to join a breakout room.

Whatever the circumstances, the first thing you need to understand is why this disengagement is happening. This may have nothing to do with you, and your positive starting point is that something understandably distracting is going on in their world. If you start out by thinking this is a result of you or your session, your mood may be impacted and so will your responses. Their issue could be something as simple as poor connectivity. Or perhaps their boss is pressurising them, a client requires an immediate response or their child is causing distractions.

In the face-to-face environment, you'd take the person to one side in a break and have a quiet discussion. The same applies in a virtual classroom. In a virtual classroom you're visible almost all of the time and everyone can see what you're saying or doing. Nobody wants a public rebuke or a group discussion about why they are disengaged, disruptive or upset.

To get to the bottom of the problem you must speak to them privately during a break, avoiding publicly questioning their behaviour and potentially turning a molehill into a mountain. You can achieve this by:

- sending a private message during a break (and double-checking before you send it that it's only going to them and not to the whole group)

- asking them a question related to your session to re-position their focus – this might be enough on its own to get them back on track
- when you put everyone in a breakout room, keeping them in the main room for a quick chat
- breaking out from the main session together for the conversation
- video-calling them or phoning in a break

It's a great idea to have a WhatsApp group (or similar closed messaging group) dedicated to the facilitating team so you can communicate outside the application you are using for the session.

TAKE CHARGE

You are the director of time and process, taking people skilfully and intuitively from start to finish. Remember that throughout your delivery. It's not just about *control*, but *responsibility*. If you don't take charge, the session will either degenerate – or someone else will take control.

USE YOUR KNOWLEDGE

Your in-depth knowledge remains the foundation of your content. Your goal is to challenge, support, share and inspire.

It's up to you to ensure participants are completely present: doing, responding, talking and being involved – *not* passively listening. You're leading an interactive experience where content or knowledge is shared, skills start to develop, behavioural change is supported and people feel inspired.

The facilitator must be able to read and respond to the concerns of participants, be authentic and act genuinely. This can be achieved through quality questions, empathic listening and directive challenge when needed. You are already familiar with this as an experienced educator. What is required is adaptation to a virtual environment.

Be prepared to use fewer words and less content, as well as employing cleaner, sharper questions. Your instructions need to be crisper and more directional than in face-to-face encounters.

It's handy to keep reminding yourself that your facial expressions are constantly on view, and online silences seem to last forever. Put a note above your webcam to smile: it will help.

Virtual facilitation is not about being a larger-than-life entertainer, telling stories and sharing a bucket-load of information – as it can be in the physical world. Rather, it's about listening and allowing participants to explore and have their conversations – about moving away from being an entertainer to a conversation facilitator. It's important to highlight that presenters who rely on charisma to influence may not be able to persuade in the same way in an online setting.

In a virtual setting, you must not only connect with people but also ensure they all have an equal voice and that there's an equal value given to everyone's perspective. When a meeting is well managed it can equalise everyone's input and can lead to more creative and satisfying outcomes. By using the chat, polling and structured methods of group interaction you can also reduce the dominance of the usual suspects: those one or two voices who can overwhelm a session.

The chat function alone is invaluable. We've all been in face-to-face meetings where you had a great idea but the moment to contribute it passes and the golden nugget is lost, sometimes forever. Most workplace environments heavily favour the world's extroverts and their needs are still met in the virtual space, but online can help some introverts to contribute more freely.

The heart of your session is still your content. It's your existing skills and experience in delivery that will still pass this on. Virtual facilitation requires subtle differences, some of which may come naturally and obviously, while others may be more nuanced.

FACILITATION ROLES: WHO'S ON YOUR TEAM?

Experienced educators who already delivering as part of a team may find some of this section basic. We aren't trying to teach people how to deliver as part of a team, or examine team dynamics, but we are attempting to prepare facilitators for the likelihood that team delivery will become one of the new norms if we are to place the learner's needs and delivery of quality outcomes at the heart of this new, blended approach to delivery.

Many experienced educators will, no doubt, be delivering sessions alone in the real world. Virtual delivery adds a layer of complexity that requires monitoring. Being responsible for delivering content, managing engagement, and monitoring learning is tough enough without the added pressure of checking the chat box, technical issues, time management, etc.

Always consider using two or more people to run virtual classes or meetings. That isn't to say you cannot run them alone, but this takes a higher level of skill and, even then, you reduce the learner's experience. This is especially true in groups of 20+ and, of course, in even larger-scale events such as conferences.

Irrespective of the number of people delivering, there are a number of roles that need to be covered:

- host/moderator/timekeeper –the glue that holds a presentation together involving multiple contributors, polls, breakout rooms, etc, and ensuring sessions run to time
- lead presenter / facilitator – delivering the content

- co-presenter(s) – optionally may provide a different voice, perspective and input
- chat manager – acknowledging chat box comments, summarising the mood of the chat and responding to chat questions
- tech support – dealing with software or hardware issues as they arise for organisers and participants

If you are new to virtual facilitation we recommend you at least have one person to work with, as combining tech with facilitation can prove challenging. Full-time online facilitators generally prefer working with other people: the support is essential and the event often flows better for participants.

THE BENEFITS OF A FACILITATION TEAM

We believe the move to a blended approach and the use of virtual facilitation is a good thing, not just a necessary one. And team delivery has an opportunity to provide positive new opportunities for the learner experience:

- It can be more enjoyable working as a team.
- Shared workload.
- Different voices, opinions and approaches.
- Assigned roles mean you can concentrate better and play to individual strengths.
- Collective knowledge for better design and delivery.
- One can deal with tech, while the other concentrates on delivery.
- If there's a tech problem, one can deal with it, while the other facilitates and keeps talking.
- One can monitor chat and reply, while the main delivery continues.
- More than one person monitoring participation levels / non-verbal cues / disengagement.
- If there's an odd number for a paired exercise, one can step in.

- Review and feedback enable more rapid improvement and development.

This isn't an exhaustive list of benefits – and some may be personal to you. In our opinion the most important factor that should drive the decision to work in a team is – a better experience for learners.

FINDING A CO-PRESENTER, BUILDING A TEAM

The benefits of working with others in virtual facilitation are great enough that we think it's a good idea to seek out people to co-present with, if that suits your style.

You could, for example, look through your contacts and find someone who *you* could help, and who might reciprocate in return. It's possible you already know someone, a supplier, or even a customer, who would be well placed to run events with you.

Create or join learning groups to share and learn and develop together. This can increase the speed of your development, and offers support.

The skills of facilitation work across industry sectors and the process of running virtual classrooms is transferrable. This creates an opportunity for educators and teachers to share insights with professional facilitators in the corporate world.

THE KEYS TO SUCCESSFUL VIRTUAL TEAM FACILITATION

Teamworking in an online environment is subtly different to working together in person. The ability for energy to bounce off each other will be reduced. There's less opportunity for the knowing glance or other non-verbal cues that people rely on when in the same room. However, the fundamentals of team presentation that many experienced facilitators will recognise still apply:

- Everyone knows their responsibilities.
- Know each other's roles, but don't overstep the mark by doing their job for them.
- Communication between organisers on a separate channel from the group.
- Stick to timings.
- Help each other out.
- Don't argue or debate – unless it's part of the plan.
- Practise before going live.
- Get your setups in sync – if you place things in similar positions on your screen it will make directing to a solution easier.
- Make sure the team has all of the presentation aids – polls, etc – to hand. If the lead presenter goes offline, can someone pick up the reins?
- Share ideas for disaster recovery so anyone can respond to problems as they arise.
- Share feedback after the event and plan this into the post-session routine.

Just as you would in a real-world environment, thorough preparation and post-evaluation are essential. Technology and physical distance, in particular, add a new dimension that will require practice to master so you can function as an effective team.

INCLUSIVITY & DISABILITY AWARENESS

When facilitating in-person we regularly consider all sorts of accessibility issues. Is there a lift if the training room is on the third floor? Do any of the participants have any access requirements? Do participants require a hearing loop? Questions of catering come up with regards to attendees' dietary requirements.

It is easy to dismiss or forget about these needs when training online; after all, it's not happening where you are, so what can you do about it? This will probably be well understood by educators who are themselves disabled, but might be overlooked by those without the same challenges.

Check access requirements with your participants well in advance – leaving it to the day to ask if anyone needs anything will be too late, especially if it requires a further technology solution that you need to integrate.
Build accessibility into your course design and choice of technology.

Accessibility isn't a box to be ticked; it needs to be at the heart of your thinking to ensure attendees have the best possible learning experience. Often, the requirement to simplify language and design to make online learning easier, is actually a key to user-friendliness. For many educators, exploring these issues may be an eye-opener and reveal improvements that can transfer to physical-world delivery.

This is a learning process for educators and learners alike. Finding ways to make content easier to absorb is important, irrespective of disability, and recognising the many challenges that learners experience.

ACCESS CONSIDERATIONS

There are a number of areas where accessibility can have an impact on your content and delivery. This section aims to be an overview of issues, and more detail can be found in the sections that follow.

ACCESS TO TECHNOLOGY

Irrespective of disability, lack of access to technology can be a major barrier to online learning. What provisions could you make to permit access via methods other than a desktop or laptop computer with a large screen? How can you grant access if the participant doesn't have a smartphone? Most video-conferencing platforms permit access via phone, but you will have to bear this in mind when delivering that not everyone will be able to see slides or comments in the chat.

Setting up the technology in the first place may be challenging, and people may need help in getting set up. Do you have any provision for such assistance?

TECHNOLOGY ADD-ONS

Consider backup platforms that you might turn to and whether an account is necessary beforehand. Does everyone need a Google, Facebook or WhatsApp account in order to participate?

Are there any add-ons to the video-conferencing platform that might be required? For example, does it offer live captioning or screen-reading? More on this in the technology section that follows.

YOUR TEAM

Are there ways in which disabled people might be involved in your events as a speaker, presenter, tech support or other form of contributor?

PHYSICAL ACCESS

An online environment may provide easier access in many respects as the participant's location may be beyond your control. Personal factors might mean that you must schedule more breaks to allow for physical or other needs.

SPEED OF DELIVERY & QUANTITY OF CONTENT

People with intellectual and developmental disabilities may need additional time to process information.

It might help participants if they can send questions in advance of the main session. If you send out the types of questions that will be asked during the session it will allow for preparation.

Consider preparing a glossary of terms and abbreviations to send out in advance to aid participants in processing what is being said.

CATERING

You are unlikely to be responsible for catering as participants aren't in your environment, rather their office or home. Unless you are arranging for food delivery during a break, this responsibility is probably non-existent. While you might not be ordering sandwiches and coffee, it is still incumbent on you to remind participants that it's OK to eat and drink. You can't really stop it anyway, but you can set the tone for the classroom, and ensure that they have refreshments on hand to aid their comfort, learning and wellbeing.

If you are running long events, you need to remind people that they will need to have food available. The last thing you need is a participant forgetting and disappearing to the shops to get supplies and returning late.

THE TECHNICAL ENVIRONMENT

Many people don't factor technology into the process until too late. As facilitators there are many decisions and choices to be made long before you run a session and there's probably more to think about than you imagine. Your hardware and software are the bedrock of your delivery – from choosing the platform to the kit you use.

AUDIO

Some facilitators prefer microphones – which is fine if you have a quiet environment, but they do tend to pick up distracting background noises. Bluetooth headphones allow you the freedom to move around, but batteries can be an issue: you may need to consider investing in a backup.

Whatever option you decide to go with, ensure you turn them off, go onto mute or unplug before you make a drink or go to the toilet, to avoid any embarrassing experiences. A reminder on the door as you leave might spare your blushes – yes, it really does happen!

Poor audio quality can make it impossible for someone with hearing impairments or sensory disabilities to continue. So, it's important that not only presenters' audio is clear, but also that of all participants.

WEBCAM

A quality webcam is crucial, as is testing it in advance.

You need to make sure you are positioned well in front of it, with the webcam roughly at eye level. If you position it so it is either looking up or down at you it will look unprofessional. Also, pay attention to the so-called 'rule of thirds' that suggests your eyeline should be about one-third down the screen.

Many devices allow you to bring up a grid that places virtual lines on the screen so you can position yourself. Don't worry, these guide lines to do not appear for the participant.

INTERNET CONNECTION

You now need to make your connection as stable as possible. Test the speed of your connection using an online speed measurement tool (easily found by searching Google). If all is well it will show you are in a good position to stream video.

But you shouldn't put all your eggs in one basket. You need a broadband backup. Connecting your computer to the hotspot on your phone if the connection fails is one solution.

If you do lose your connection, step one is... don't panic. Dropping off online platforms is virtually a way of life for some part and everyone is getting very used to it. Step two is to try to get back in using your pre-arranged backup plan.

If that doesn't work, either reboot or have a second device you can connect with to hand – even if it's only a tablet, you can still get back in and manage the situation.

You could also try plugging your device directly into the router and hardwire your connection to overcome issues that are to do with the wi-fi. Cabled connections are faster than wi-fi, so this is good practice in general, if you can route cables safely between your router and computer.

As a last resort, disconnect your video and just use audio to save bandwidth and see if that makes a difference.

Remember that corporate networks must be secure, which means that they can sometimes be slower than home broadband connections. Also, people in remote parts of a country can find their connections slower than elsewhere.

VIDEO-CONFERENCING PLATFORMS

To get 100% comfortable with the platform you're using, sign up as a participant and experience it from that perspective. See what works, what engages you – and what doesn't.

Another practical tip is to log on with a second device, mute the sound so there's no feedback and check out what it looks like from your participants' perspective.

With regards to the platform(s) you choose, this may come down to your personal choice, but will just as likely be down to the client or employer and their policies and hardware and software choices. *Your* choice can be based on features, security, cost and ease of use.

With different platforms, browsers and devices, functionality isn't identical across all video-conferencing solutions.

Also, technology is moving at such a pace that any recommendations we make today will probably be outdated in a month's time. However, we've included a list of platforms and tools you may wish to investigate. There will be increasing competition in this space to provide services that meet customers' demands – customers like us who want to deliver online learning. It's a safe bet that there will be solutions available in a year's time that will be better than those around today. For example, while writing and publishing this book (over approximately three months) Google launched video conferencing embedded in their calendar app, and Zoom went from 10 million to 200 million users (and is still growing).

We're not on commission, so there's no bias or prejudice involved, and we're acutely aware that it's far from a complete list as technology is moving on very quickly. With that caveat, here are some video-conferencing platforms worth considering:

- Adobe Connect
- AnyMeeting
- BigBlueButton
- Blackboard Collaborate
- BlueJeans
- Cisco Jabber
- Cisco Webex Meetings

- ezTalks
- Fuze
- GlobalMeet Collaboration
- Google Hangouts and Google Meet
- GoToMeeting
- Jitsi
- join.me
- Lifesize
- Microsoft Teams
- ON24
- Polycom
- Skype
- TeamViewer
- UberConference
- Whereby
- Zoho Meeting
- Zoom

Here are two (of many) sites that compare platforms. The second has a focus on accessibility. Be aware when using these sites that their opinions might be influenced by the rewards they get (or don't) when you click on a link and purchase:

- www.webconferencing-test.com
- https://bighack.org/best-videoconferencing-apps-and-software-for-accessibility

COLLABORATION TOOLS

The following collaboration tools can help you to collaborate with your team through a central hub for sharing information:

- Blackboard Collaborate
- eXo Platform
- Huddle
- Lighthouse

- Mentimeter
- Microsoft Teams
- Podio
- Redbooth
- Slack
- Webex Teams
- Zoho Connect

FILE-SHARING PLATFORMS

You might also consider file-sharing platforms that allow you to co-create and co-edit documents or visuals in real-time with your team:

- Conceptboard
- Google Docs
- ONLYOFFICE
- Prezi
- Scribblar
- Xtensio

Not all file formats are accessible. For information on legal requirements and best practice for publishing online, visit:

www.gov.uk/government/publications/inclusive-communication/accessible-communication-formats

COMMUNICATIONS & MESSAGING

You probably use a variety of means of communicating with your participants. It's important to consider whether they require an account, hardware, or software before they can use them. If this is the case, ensure everyone is set up in advance. Consider how accessible these methods are, and how receptive participants are to their use.

- Email
- Text
- Telephone

- Facebook Messenger
- Facebook Live
- Google Hangouts
- Instagram Live/Stories
- WhatsApp

ACCESSIBILITY ADD-ONS

There are many options for add-on solutions to improve accessibility. These include:

- Braille translators and printers emboss information onto heavyweight paper.
- Braille notetakers for storing notes, web browsing, storing contacts and appointments and replay via synthesizer or braille. The name belies the scope of their functionality.
- Captions can be added to videos and live captioning can be incorporated into presentations using software or professional captioning services.
- Deafblind communication systems such as FaceToFace and FSTTY allow deafblind and sighted people to communicate.
- Digital talking book players (hardware and software) turn text to speech and allow users to navigate through a book.
- Educational technology customised to certain applications exist to support people with a variety of disabilities. These include talking or large-display calculators, large-print keyboards, over-sized mice, talking tactile tablets and other learning aids.
- GPS- (global positioning system) enabled devices to navigate may be keyboard or voice operated.
- Low vision optical devices help visually impaired users by magnifying objects and improving illumination.

- Optical character recognition (OCR) converts print to text and text to speech, while applying contextual rules to make sense where the scan might be unclear.

- Screen magnification is built into most monitors and software programs so users can change the size of text and images.

- Screen readers allow blind and visually impaired users to hear on-screen text via a speech synthesizer or braille display.

- Signing allows hearing-impaired attendees to understand speech, and requires a competent signer to be available on screen at all times.

- Speech synthesizers in the form of built-in cards in computers, plug-in hardware or software produce increasingly realistic human voices.

- Ultrasound devices can provide auditory or vibrating feedback as users approach objects.

- Video magnifiers project magnified images onto a computer or television screen.

- Voice-recognition technology is being increasingly integrated into products and can provide speech-to-text capabilities.

The most important question will be whether the video conferencing platform in use is compatible with the assistive technology.

MULTIPLE SCREENS

If you have a wide screen or two-screen setup, keep a copy of the notes on your desktop so you can cut and paste documents, questions, and comments easily from chat boxes to update your session.

PRACTISE USING DIFFERENT HARDWARE

Never assume that what *you're* seeing on your screen is necessarily what *they're* seeing on theirs. The screen setup changes depending on the tech they are using; the view and the tools are in different places if you are on a desktop, tablet, phone or other device.

If you want the participants to see their screen in a specific view, always let them know. I recommend asking members to choose 'side-by-side' gallery view, so that if there are ten people on the call, you see all ten people, not five. You, as facilitator, want to be able to see everyone and you want to focus your observational energy on your participants. It's also worth considering 'double-screen' delivery so you can show slides while being aware of how people are responding.

Understanding participants' level of tech-savviness is critical. You might have people new to live virtual working, people who are great with technology but not used to the specific system, and people who need much less support. If you can gauge their level of expertise by chatting to them or perhaps by doing a poll, this will help you to know the level at which you can pitch the tech side of things.

It's also helpful to feed back the results to the group, so those less experienced know that they're not alone. For example, you can say: '50% of you are totally new to this and 30% have only experienced this platform occasionally – while 20% understand the tools and are very experienced. So, I'm just going to go through the basics very briefly.'

Help allay any concerns they might have by putting the phone number of the person running the technology into the chat and alert every participant that it's there, just in case they have problems with their access to the meeting or their use of the system: 'If you get disconnected, please call Jamie. His number is at the top of the chat, and he'll get you back into the session.'

Leading by example is also good. So, if you're getting group members to draw, write or stamp onto slides or whiteboards, if you prime your co-host to kick-start the process by writing in the chat first, or annotating the slides or whatever, this will encourage others to follow. People often dislike being the first to do a task, but they will more happily follow when someone leads the way.

TOP TIPS

WEBCAM

- A good quality webcam is crucial for clarity of image.
- Position your webcam so your eyes are one third of the way from the top of the screen – looking up or down at it can compromise your authority.

HEADSETS

- Bluetooth headphones allow freedom of movement.
- Make sure your headphones are fully charged and you have spare batteries.
- Switch off or mute your headphones if you leave the room while still wearing them.
- Corded rather than wireless headphones offer better quality and consistency.

MICROPHONE

- Free-standing microphones work well in quiet environments but will pick up background noises.
- Have a backup microphone.

INTERNET

- Have a backup broadband connection in case your primary service fails.
- Your phone hotspot can work well as a back-up.
- If you experience wireless connectivity issues, try connecting directly to your router (before the session starts).

- If you are still having problems in-session disconnect your video to save bandwidth.
- Invest in a wi-fi range extender to boost the signal around your house or office.

EXTENDING SCREEN SIZE

- Use a widescreen monitor or two screens to switch between video calls and source material and have more of your resources readily to hand.

POSITIONING

- Your screen and webcam should be positioned so that you are central and making eye contact.
- Your eyeline should be one-third of the way from the top of the screen.
- Devices will allow you to put virtual grids across the screen showing you where to position yourself without showing to participants.

PLATFORM

- Choose a platform based on functionality, security, accessibility, cost and ease of use.
- Sign up to the platform you'll be using as a guest to experience it from another perspective.

TEST, TEST, TEST

- Test everything, more than once.
- Log in with a second device to view your setup from the perspective of your participants.

PARTICIPANTS / TEAM

- Consider running pre-session training to familiarise participants with the technology.
- Provide tips-sheets on using the technology.

- Have someone on hand to refer to on accessibility issues.

THE PHYSICAL
ENVIRONMENT

WHAT'S BEHIND YOU?

Look at what's behind you when you're on screen and avoid clutter. Fire up your webcam and pay close attention to what your participants will see. Ideally, there should be something pleasant to look at – perhaps flowers, a photo or piece of art. You need to create a pleasant environment, but not a distracting one.

Of course, it comes down to personal choice. Do you want a virtual background with a personal connection or your own natural backdrop, so people get a real-life insight into your environment? This will depend on your style. Some experts think that using virtual backdrops or blank screens removes distractions, while others believe that participants want to see the authentic you, so that they can understand you better. Ultimately, you need to consider what story your background is saying about you, and make it a conscious choice rather than using something just because you can.

LIGHTING

Unless you have a very high-quality HD camera, small patterns on fabric may get blurred on the screen (strobing, in broadcast parlance), while reading glasses will reflect light onto the screen, unless you have non-reflective lenses. Lighting must be strong, without being blinding or distracting, and usually in front of you to avoid casting shadows. The main light source should be in front of you and your screen. If it is behind you then you risk being little more than a silhouette.

If you have any doubts, ask a colleague for an opinion on how you look on screen.

VIRTUAL BACKGROUNDS

If you choose to use a virtual background we recommend you use a green screen: otherwise you risk the background distorting. Test it with what you intend wearing. Green screen works by eliminating a colour (normally green, but some work on other colours) from the screen. So, if you are wearing a green top, then your body will disappear too: very distracting!

Even if you do select a virtual background, make sure your backdrop is clutter-free. If, for any reason, the virtual background doesn't work, the default will be what's in your room.

Test, test, test your virtual backgrounds before using them for real.

CLEAR YOUR DESK

Before you start, you need to clear your physical desk of unnecessary distractions. This should also reduce the risk of knocking items over or of not being able to find something you want to physically share.

Put your phone away to avoid unwanted calls or messages, along with the temptation to sneakily check emails or social media. People always notice this. Don't have it on silent with vibrate on as it's going to buzz away on your desk and distract – unless it is an essential part of your technology delivery plan.

You may consider a desk with adjustable height, so you can either sit or stand. If seated, ensure you are facing the screen, with good posture: your bottom back in the chair, both your feet on the ground, your spine straight and your shoulders back.

Consider having a copy of your notes or lesson plan with clear, minute-by-minute timings and slides on a stand next to your screen so you can check progress unobtrusively.

Have your participant register within reach, so you not only know people by name but can also demonstrate understanding about their roles and backgrounds. This will help you feel focused on human beings, rather than names on a screen.

MOVING AROUND THE ROOM

When facilitating a workshop in person, many choose to stand, which helps to project the voice and give more freedom of movement. This applies to online facilitation; however, whatever style you choose, remember the advice on positioning your webcam and the rule of thirds. You will lose the impact of facial expressions if you move away from the camera.

TOP TIPS

- Your desk and surroundings should be clear of anything that could distract you.
- Make sure participants see what you *want* them to see; they will focus on your background during a video call.
- Virtual backdrops can negate distractions, while natural backdrops give a real-life insight into you and your environment. Decide what serves you best.
- Switch off your phone or leave it out of earshot to prevent unwanted calls or messages, as well as the temptation to check notifications.
- Consider adjusting the height of your desk or screen for comfort, ease of use and visibility.
- Standing during a workshop can help to project your voice and offer greater range of movement.
- Remaining seated requires good posture to portray a confident and energised persona.

- Have both physical and digital notes easily available to remind yourself of key points, without being obvious.
- Keep participants' names and webcams in view so you focus on people, not just your slides and the technology.
- Adjust the lighting to prevent glare and shadows and provide even lighting.
- Check the lighting for the time you are delivering – if you practise during the day there will be natural light, but as night falls you'll be relying on artificial lights.
- The main light source should be in front of you – if it is behind you it will cause shadows.

CONTENT DESIGN

DESIGN TIME

One aspect of virtual facilitation that few anticipate is just how much time you need in preparation. You need to schedule time to think about the system design – not just the learning design. On average, it takes three or four times longer to design a virtual session than a face-to-face one – and as much as six times longer when inexperienced.

If you are just starting out, allow 6–10 hours of preparation for each hour of virtual content. Experienced facilitators will find they can plan a new project from scratch in 4–6 hours. It's not a quick process.

A decent chunk of that time will not be creating content… but discarding it. As much as 80% of the core content you'd probably use face-to-face will need to be condensed or cut. As a guide, you'll only need 20% of the content you might have used face-to-face. It's almost always about cutting content from your original design. It's *very* rare that a facilitator finds they've put in too little material.

CREATIVE DESIGN OF AN ONLINE SESSION

Now, let's look at the techniques: the practical tips and best practice involved in designing things creatively.

Very often people start off by either combining too many different technologies, or trying to wow people with technology. Over time we've all learned that tends to distract from the purpose of the session. We can probably all relate to seeing a presentation where the presenter has gone overboard on using animations and transitions. As is true so often online, less is more. Your focus needs to be on creating the right environment and having conversations that identify priorities and facilitate outcomes. That is what will keep people interested and engaged, not bells and whistles.

DESIGN CONSIDERATIONS

Next comes the content. What guides the achievement of the purpose and outcomes of the session?

1. Purpose & Outcomes
2. Structure
3. Reduce
4. Energise
5. Reflect
6. Be punctual
7. Engage
8. Be visual

#1 PURPOSE & OUTCOMES

The key question you need to ask is 'Why?' Are you clear on the purpose of your session, what you want to achieve, who is it for and what do you want them to take away? In other words, what will success look like?

Once you've decided that, you can choose what you communicate so that participants feel energised and aligned to the outcomes. Remember, it is all about the participants and what they need.

- Why you are delivering *this* session?
- Who it is for?
- What do you want them to achieve?
- What do you want to achieve for yourself?

This purpose must be communicated so that participants feel energised and aligned to the outcomes.

#2 STRUCTURE

What could be placed outside the virtual classroom using a blended approach (live and online training), before, during or after the workshop? This could be learning that is self-managed by the participants, for example. If you are using a blended approach or an extended programme, what is the format?

Is the content broken down in a modular approach in a logical sequence so the learners can see the whole journey through the programme?

What is the duration? Two hours, once a week, for six weeks is a very successful longer-term format. A more immersive experience over two days is another option. Alternatively, this could run for three hours, bi-weekly, for six weeks.

- Can you break down the programme into modules so that participants view it as a journey?
- Should I use intensive delivery to offer an immersive experience?

If you consider the duration, your blended approach and the self-directed elements of learning, you will provide a valuable experience.

#3 REDUCE

What are the most valuable elements that will deliver the outcomes and engage participants? What could be reduced or cut? This includes reducing content and the number of desired outcomes, as well as the amount of technology you use. Using other technologies and tools can very useful (and makes a welcome change), but keep people inside one application as much as possible. Every time you use other technologies, track onto other websites or start using other tools you're creating a temptation for participants to linger there or go further afield to check other resources, or worse, their emails.

#4 ENERGISE

How many breaks need to be included to ensure energy levels are maintained and how long should the session run? Timings are crucial for any facilitation, but the importance of timing doubles when it's virtual. Shorter sessions are required.

What's the optimum number of hours for delegates to learn virtually or to be in a meeting per day? One, two or three hours is the answer. Yes, you *can* do more (and you probably *will*, when you really must), but participants, as well as you, will suffer and feel drained, rather than enthused and energised to come back.

From experience, 90 minutes is often the sweet spot.

#5 REFLECT

Ask yourself what opportunities you are building in for reflective learners either before, during or after the session. Just as in the physical room, the design may include plenary and small group / breakout sessions. Our aim is for 65% of the time to be experiential with participants interacting and collaborating.

Lecture-style delivery will hold attention for far less time online than face-to-face. It's essential to build in interactivity, and in so doing you add time to the content. This is one reason so much content has to be stripped from an existing session plan.

#6 BE PUNCTUAL

One of the biggest shifts that the virtual world brings is the absolute requirement to plan and practise your sessions down to the last detail. And this really does mean *to the minute.*

Face-to-face training allows you to adapt your structure as you progress to some extent. There's an opportunity to go off-piste and return to the plan according to the needs of participants.

In the virtual environment you need to stick to your timings. Set reminders so you hit each next section on time. Factor in 5–10 minutes of contingency time per 60 minutes of content. A dalliance online can seriously throw out your timings.

#7 ENGAGE

Ask yourself: after a break would *you* come back to the session you have designed? You need to keep things interactive and full of variety to ensure delegates are engaged, the session feels fresh and they want to return. If participants are doing too much listening they will disengage. In a virtual meeting, someone speaking for twenty minutes without breaks is just awful. Participants need to be doing something – roughly every 3–5 minutes. This could be giving feedback, voting, taking part in breakouts or drawing or writing on whiteboards.

Vary the pace with a mixture of energetic activities and time to reflect. This reflects the importance of a creative and varied design. Shorter sessions with more frequent interaction mean materials and instructions must be much simpler.

#8 BE VISUAL

If your slides and props aren't punchy, visual and gripping go back to the drawing board. Use imagery, audio and video, while keeping the total number of slides as low as possible. If you are showing a video clip remember to keep them to no longer than 2–3 minutes, as this is the maximum length you'll keep people engaged.

Emotional responses can aid memory, so photos or videos that are funny, moving or trigger memories are most effective. Getting participants to annotate slides or whiteboards helps to increase engagement and is a great way of capturing learning.

DESIGNING YOUR SLIDES FOR ONLINE ENGAGEMENT

- Maximise the use of visuals, such as photos and icons. These work as memory triggers. Words are there just to emphasise and reinforce.
- Keep your word count low to avoid overcrowding and increase the impact of your messages.

- Highlight one main point on each slide, with three to five (maximum) sub-points for explanations.
- Remove banners, logos, headers and footers to make your slides cleaner.
- Page numbering can help everyone to navigate and ask to see a slide again if they missed it or need to review its content.
- Make text and visuals as large as possible to make them easy to view on different screens: don't assume everyone is using a desktop; they might be using a laptop, tablet or even their mobile phone.
- Use simple, easy-to-read fonts.
- Use plain language.
- Avoid ableist language (see www.selfdefined.app for advice on terms to avoid or use with caution).
- Consider using images instead of words.
- If you have attendees with visual impairments, remember to describe images so they know what everyone else is looking at.
- Avoid anything that strobes or flashes (either in videos or images). If you have to use, warn beforehand.
- If an image is key to your lesson, fill an entire slide with it and only place descriptive text at the top.
- Make sure the background colour makes text legible.
- Add animations that reveal parts of each slide as you narrate them (rather than showing everything on the slide at once).
- Use bold type or bold colours to highlight key words and points.

FREE IMAGES TO BOOST YOUR SLIDES

Copyright is important, and should be respected. Here are some sources of copyright-free and royalty-free images you can use in your presentations. There are many more, and some may be better suited if your needs are niche.

- flikr.com
- freepik.com
- pexels.com
- rawpixel.com

STAYING ON SCHEDULE

Getting participants to stick to a schedule – especially in large numbers – can be a challenge. One way to help people to get back on time from breaks or breakouts is to broadcast the same song a few minutes before they're expected to be return. It should become familiar to them and an automatic call to return, particularly if you work with the same group over many sessions. Make a note to play it to them when you're dealing with the ground rules.

BREAKS

The longest period online that is effective without a break is 90 minutes. Two hours also works. You *can* push it to three hours, but you need a proper refreshments and personal needs break.

Some of the most effective sessions are delivered in 90 minutes, then 60 minutes break for refreshments and personal needs, followed by another 90 minutes.

Generally, the longer the session, the more critical it is to allow for reflection. This can be enabled by giving participants the opportunity to get up and walk away from their desk or for some related activity – perhaps to complete a questionnaire or do a 'pair walk'. A pair walk is really effective and is where two participants video chat directly with each other on their phone and go for a *physical* walk together – round their respective gardens, houses or streets – discussing what they believe is the key priority for their team. This allows them to engage physically as well as mentally. Participants really appreciate this variety and it raises energy levels.

Effective participant engagement is not so different online as it is in physical sessions. In fact, whatever works for you in-person you can generally adapt to suit this environment, from videos to showing clips, using humour, music, case studies, etc.

TIME ZONES

If you are working internationally, it's obviously crucial to time your meeting to match the needs of as many participants as possible – and to explain the reason for the timings during the session. This enables you to graciously acknowledge those people who might have sacrificed their meal time, or their sleep, to attend. Bear in mind not only the start time, but finish times in the time zones you'll be serving.

KEYS TO PARTICIPANT ENGAGEMENT

When you're designing your sessions, there are some great ways to make sure you keep the energy up and the participants' attention on the job at hand. Obviously, the type of event you are hosting and the number of participants will dictate what you can and can't take advantage of. Here are some of our favourites:

USE PEOPLE'S NAMES

Keep acknowledging people by name, especially in the chat. Even if you're not going to ask them about their comments, simply by doing this you're acknowledging them and keeping the engagement going. People respond positively to just hearing their name called out and their contributions noticed.

If you spot that someone hasn't spoken for a while you can either say, 'Louise, it'd be good to hear from you on this', or 'I'd like to hear from someone who hasn't spoken for a while. Let's see… Anneliese, what occurs to you in terms of marketing?' This gives Anneliese two clues you are about to ask her a question. Believe me, she'll be grateful!

I also strongly recommend checking in with people at regular intervals – no matter the size of the group. You could ask: 'How does that idea sound to everyone? Thumbs up if you're fine with it.'

Alternatively, pick out those who disagree by asking everyone to cover their camera if they do agree with you, leaving a small number still showing who disagree, whom you can then engage with. You can also use the more nuanced 'high, medium or low' reaction, with members putting their hands at the top, centre or low part of the screen. This allows you to see their levels of engagement.

If you risk an open question like 'Does anyone have anything to add?' in a real-world scenario, it can work brilliantly: you can normally sense who has more to say. Unluckily, this works badly online. Online, 95% of the time what you get is a whopping silence, which feels awkward for everyone. For this reason, requesting that people use chat to add a point generally works better. We recommend using your co-facilitator to interject. 'Hey James, excuse me, but I have an excellent comment from Mae here.'

Always tell participants what to do with their answers whenever you ask a question – is it unmute and speak, or in the chat box, or some other way?

To get maximum engagement, a great combination is to start with a closed question – for example: 'Who finds giving negative feedback difficult?' and raise your own hand to encourage participation, and then pick someone with a raised hand: 'Olivia, let's start with you. Please share what you personally find difficult.'

It's worth bearing in mind that if you have participants with sensory disabilities, if people speak over each other this may cause avoidable confusion. A way of reducing this confusion is by asking attendees to say their name before speaking.

ENGAGEMENT ACTIVITIES

Many of the activities you use in the real world work online, too. The following lists are intended be a prompt to help you mix activities and participant responses into your session, in addition to your own tried and tested activities.

- case studies
- video (max 3 minutes)
- audio / music
- images on-screen
- hold up physical objects to the webcam
- slides
- screen sharing

- use a pointer to highlight a relevant point on screen
- physically moving around your office
- flipchart behind you and to one side on camera
- breakout rooms
- check-in
- ask questions to the group
- ask questions to individuals
- annotate key points as you present
- ask people to write something down

PARTICIPANT RESPONSES

- hands up (physically)
- thumbs-up response
- round of applause
- write in chat
- fill in a document
- respond to poll
- participants pair up and walk and talk
- peer coaching
- action learning for problem solving
- reflection time
- solo presentation
- mini-group presentations
- get up, move around
- virtual whiteboard
- fishbowl with focus on 2–3 people
- write notes

POLLS

If the platform you are using has polls this can be a brilliant engagement feature. It lets you:

- Gather feedback to gauge participant understanding before starting a topic.

- Gain immediate feedback to help identify learning issues.
- Change the monotony of a meeting or session by breaking up the content flow.
- Stimulate discussion via open-ended inquiries where everyone has an equal voice.
- Check understanding using closed questions.
- Quickly evaluate and gain feedback on how the session is going / has gone.

WHITEBOARDS

Many platforms have whiteboards. Writing something down, or drawing it on a virtual whiteboard, helps improve ideas, memory and collaboration. If you don't have this functionality, remember there is always the old-school option of having a flip chart in the view of the webcam that you can physically use to capture ideas or share content.

FISHBOWLS / HOT SEATS

A fishbowl or hot seat is where everyone listens in to two or three people having a conversation. The benefit of this activity is it offers focus and an opportunity to deepen the conversation rather than separating into smaller groups. It gives the facilitator the opportunity to give certain participants a reason to speak and others to practise active listening – a useful skill as well an opportunity to observe and learn from how others interact.

If you do this you must remember in your design process to include a step where everyone else turns off their webcam and presses 'hide non-video participants'. This will help everyone to focus on the people speaking. Also, loads of empty screens is not a great look.

BREAKOUT ROOMS

Some platforms offer breakout rooms or breakout channels. This is where many of the quality conversations happen, because they are places where people feel less guarded or under scrutiny. Groups of 3–5 people tend to work best, depending on the duration of the session and the desired outcomes. Often, the first breakout is a chance for participants to introduce themselves to each other: you therefore need to allow an extra couple of minutes as part of the first breakout for this to happen.

How many breakouts do you need?

In a 90-minute session we recommend two breakouts of 10–30 minutes, depending on the depth of the tasks and the numbers in each group. Obviously, the more people involved, the more time will be required.

As the facilitator, you have two choices:

- Go to the breakout room (assuming delegates have been told that this will happen) and either observe or join the discussion.
- Not attend the breakout rooms at all, enabling members to have their own confidential space.

It's never a good idea to drop into breakout rooms midway, unless you have agreed this will happen, as this interrupts the flow and disrupts conversations.

If you don't join the breakout, the best solution is to let everybody know you can be called upon, but won't just turn up. They can call you in if they need you. *They* are in control.

The instructions for every breakout discussion need to be explicit and agreed. The minute people go off to the breakout rooms their focus changes. Putting the questions and any documents they're going to need into the chat can really help. You can also encourage them to take a photo or screenshot of the screen.

Some platforms allow participants to download a document with instructions, which can be useful if the instructions are long. Remember though, if you send an attachment in the comments, don't assume everyone has been able to access it. It's wise to check everyone has received them and read them.

You must also clearly communicate the requirements for feedback. Ideally, one person ought to be responsible for relaying the key points, themes or insights arising during the breakout to the full group. This is to avoid the confusion of choosing a spokesperson afterwards. Someone else could volunteer to be a scribe, and another to do the timekeeping, if required.

You need to be clear about the length of time available for feedback. What you really don't want is for one person to speak for 10–15 minutes. Not only will this put you behind schedule, but it won't help to build consensus and engagement. And it's also unfair to the rest of the group and to anyone who now won't have time to give feedback because you have to cut them short.

All breakout groups should begin the session with a clear understanding that you're looking for 1–2 minutes feedback, or three strong insights or top two tips: headlines, not essays.

If you are looking to mix up the groups in the second breakout session you will need to either prepare this in advance or randomly assign people twice. Either way you need to be prepared.

Consider what you are going to do when participants are in breakout rooms. While they are doing activities, you can use that time effectively to review which participants haven't spoken yet or who has been less active on chat, and how you will involve them. Plan and adjust the session going forward and, if necessary, consider using the contingency time you have built in to get back on schedule and review participants' needs and engagement.

How many breakout rooms you schedule will, of course, depend on the schedule. In 90 minutes, I'd recommend two breakouts; with two hours, either three or four; if the session is over three hours in duration, I prefer four. However, it's all about your preferences, your clients' needs, the group size and the subjects you are discussing.

WELCOME BACK

Have a ritual to signal participants to return from breakouts. Often, they will be in mid-conversation and all off mute, so saying 'welcome back' in a clear voice and immediately asking everyone to re-mute sends the signal that you are back in charge and ready to start with the feedback. This also avoids having to interrupt the first spokesperson to ask someone to mute who has forgotten when returning. If necessary, some platforms allow you to 'mute all'. To avoid causing offence, announce clearly if you are about to mute everyone, and why. If it becomes routine, then the group will accept this as normal. If it goes unexplained, or isn't consistent, some people will be confused and/or irritated.

QUESTIONS, AND HOW TO ASK THEM

In large groups you need to get used to saying something and getting no reaction, since you're likely to have put them all on mute. At first, this can be horribly off-putting and energy draining; we're so used to seeing people's reactions, the nods, the smiles, the little grunts of agreement and engagement. Suddenly, *that's all disappeared!* Instead, you're going to have to trust that people can hear you, trust that they're engaged and trust that your design is working. At the same time, you need to be wary of silence. If you aren't getting the reactions you expect, it could be because the participants are doing too much listening, or aren't sure what they should be doing. Remember, you need to keep this interactive and have them doing *something* every 2–3 minutes if you can.

DISENGAGEMENT – THE DANGER SIGNS

It's tougher to accurately gauge this than you might think. In the virtual world your view is limited and you lose context. For example, someone may not be looking at their screen but this isn't necessarily an indicator of disengagement. They might be making notes, or looking at some they've previously made. There may be any number of reasons they're looking away, including using two screens. At first this can be off-putting, but you have to assume they are involved and trust that your design is creating the engagement you are looking for.

There are better measures of disengagement. Here are some warning signs you shouldn't miss:

- Chat activity reduces.
- Participants stop volunteering to answer questions.
- Participants turn off their webcam.
- Participants leave the meeting altogether.
- It is clear that participants are completing irrelevant activities such as answering emails.

These actions send you a signal that you need to do things differently. You need to act. 'I notice four people have turned their webcams off, so perhaps now would be a good time to check if anyone is having any issues and a review about where we go from here.'

Similarly, you must pay attention to, and act upon, unsaid or missing messages. For example, a response like 'No, no, never mind, it doesn't matter anyway' could mean that someone wants to say something, but can no longer be bothered. You have to judge whether you wish to gently ask the person to explain what they meant or whether it might be wiser to let it go.

There can also be hostility between participants, especially if you happen to have one with radically different ideas to the majority. It's even more important to give everyone a chance to hear and understand differing perspectives, as well as the time and freedom to comment. But beware the vocal minority – sometimes a minority opinion can gain a disproportionate amount of attention and time because it is voiced louder and for longer.

To keep people on board in the virtual world you will have to be clearer and explain to participants that learning often comes from the group, from people's shared experiences, stories, articles and the conversations where they challenge, confirm, agree and agree to disagree. You will need to focus the content, and design the process, so you are a conversationalist and not a lecturer.

If you notice any of these signals, you must act, otherwise you run the risk of losing individuals and perhaps the whole group.

- Speak up and acknowledge what is happening.
- Revisit why the session is important.
- Revisit rules of attendance – participation and attention being part of that.
- If necessary, ask for an honest review of the session and the direction they would like it to proceed. You might not follow this to the letter, but at least their opinion has been heard and it might influence the rest of the session.
- Ask those who appear confused or disheartened for their perspective to give everyone a chance to engage with your session.

PRE-EVENT
PREPARATION

It takes a lot longer to prepare for virtual delivery. There's no magic bullet; you will have to put in more effort than you would when delivering in-person. You must think about every aspect of technology, design, systems, environment, delivery, skills, etc, well in advance of delivery. This will become easier and quicker with experience.

NO SUCH THING AS 'UNEXPECTED'

The one thing you can expect in the virtual world is the unexpected *will* happen. Technology is increasingly reliable but you need to accept that it will go wrong at some stage. You will probably have experienced the energy drain from people in a virtual format when technology fails.

You need to know precisely how you're going to react and what you are going to say, in advance. You also need to agree with your team what roles you'll play and how you'll respond. Having backup plans will give you the confidence to deal with the unexpected, and to maintain authority. The more natural you are, and if you've pre-planned how to respond in these scenarios, the less embarrassing they will be.

What follows is a short list of possible issues that could disrupt your session – and suggested remedies. It is not exhaustive, but it is intended to get you thinking about how you can pre-empt these issues from completely halting your session. And if something does stop it in its tracks, what you can do about that, too.

OK, so there is no way of predicting *every* variable, and listing everything that could go wrong could lead to a very long and tedious list of the unlikely to the near-impossible. So, the following examples are to get your mind focused on solving problems before they arise. One way of looking at this is to review everything in this book and ask the question: 'What if that went wrong?' Then, consider your options and plan accordingly.

In many cases, Plan B requires that you communicate clearly with participants about the alternative arrangements. This is at the heart of managing the unexpected – quickly and clearly letting everyone know what is going to happen.

TECHNOLOGY

- Headset breaks – have a second set.
- Batteries run out for wireless device – spare batteries on your desk, or use your backup device.
- Loss of internet connection – have an alternative means of connecting.
- How to run the meeting without slides – send everyone a set of slides so you can all follow along together, or use a different online collaboration platform to share slides.
- How to run the meeting without the built-in chat facility – use an alternative messaging platform.

In addition:

- Any critical hardware – have a replacement.
- Have every relevant document already attached to a group email, available to send to participants within minutes of a major breakdown in technology.
- Test everything before you start.

ENVIRONMENT

- Interrupted by doorbell – it's your choice to answer or not.
- A child or pet comes into the room, onto your lap or into camera shot – embrace the situation. This is

every child-carer's and pet-owner's reality when working from home. Show you are a compassionate parent or pet owner first and foremost; it creates the best impression.

- An alarm goes off – acknowledge it, and act on it.
- Persistent background noise such as building work next door – use a headset mic to cut out most of the background noise for people listening.

Prepare for interruptions. A note on your door might be enough to keep other people away, but don't assume this to be the case. Pets, of course, don't read notes. Plan what to say so you can take it in your stride.

DELIVERY TEAM

- One of the facilitators falls ill – ensure you have cover is someone can't make it.
- You desperately need to leave temporarily – the team covers for you; or if working alone, have an exercise ready that you can ask them to complete.

COMPLETE FAIL

What do you do if you simply cannot continue the session? Have an email/message for everyone already prepared in your drafts box with an alternative video-conferencing platform ready to switch to, and a meeting room and invite link ready to send.

PUT IN THE TIME

Spend some time adding to this list – what else could go wrong? What can come up in your experience when delivering face-to-face? Can you apply the same remedies online? Are there issues that might be more relevant to your content or situation that need to be considered?

HELPING YOUR PARTICIPANTS

Now, look at this, but apply the scenarios to *your participants*. How can you help them to overcome their problem? They aren't immune from many of the same things going wrong at their end, and they probably haven't considered contingencies like you have.

PROPER PREPARATION

Record your early or practice sessions to learn what you need to work on most. This massively contributes to your development and will accelerate your expertise in leading virtual sessions. Review how you may make use of mannerisms (verbal and physical), gestures and body language to engage with participants. How did you pace your event, did you move naturally and make eye contact with your webcam to help your participants feel listened to?

Practise your content so that you know it inside out. You can then focus on your presentation and delivery.

Prepare yourself physically, mentally and emotionally. Remind yourself you have prepared for the challenges you may face, you know your content and you are ready to enjoy the experience.

Always do a run-through with the technology you're using, immediately before the session. You should do this in the meeting room you're planning to use and with the slides and tools you've already prepared. Although tech disasters are infrequent (and are mostly due to forces beyond your control) you still need to be ready. We have experienced the frustration of days of preparation, only to find something happens on the day to disrupt the event. The more we prepare, the easier this is to overcome.

CRISIS REVEALS CHARACTER & SHAPES YOUR CREDIBILITY

If you are ready in moments of crisis your credibility will grow in the eyes of your participants. These are the moments of truth when they see how professional you are. If things go wrong: *don't* try to hide it, *do* let your participants know what's happening and *do* communicate confidence in your backup plans. If you do, they'll understand, empathise and, hopefully, even admire you a little bit more!

GETTING THE INVITE RIGHT

Your welcome starts well before the event itself. What's the right tone for your invite? Is it formal? Or is it: 'Bring a cup of coffee, something comfortable to wear and a sandwich.' The more informal and relaxed you appear to be, the more approachable you'll seem. You're setting the scene so, hopefully, they'll *look forward* to coming to the session.

While the tone is down to your particular event, your invite will usually need to introduce:

- your background, experience, expertise, etc.
- what the session is going to cover, together with timings, outcomes, boundaries and expectations
- the importance of the session and of *their* attendance and contributions
- the technology or technologies you are going to be using
- any steps you'd like them to take in advance: looking at documents or videos; checking their internet connection is good; checking their audio and video work well; and so on
- any permissions you need: for example, agreement to record the meeting so ideas and conversations can be easily shared with colleagues

If you do this then participants will feel that they know, like and even trust you before they have even arrived in the virtual meeting-place.

Think about what medium you will use to deliver these messages. Are you sending the invite in writing or by video? Writing an email is obviously the traditional way of doing things, although it might be an invite link and a personal note in a Facebook Group or another social media messaging system. Sending a video clip (or a link to a video clip) increases the likelihood of the participants doing any pre-learning required. It also allows the thoughtful, more reflective type of learner to feel prepared. Reflective learners can sometimes struggle with the swift-paced, interactive cut-and-thrust of the live virtual framework, as the shortened timeframes better suit those who act on the spot.

Before you send a video, make sure the participant can receive it (big files often bounce back or are blocked by security programs). If it is a link, make sure the participant can access it where they are and on the hardware they're using (some companies place stringent restrictions on internet access). Make sure there's a way of checking that everyone has seen it – maybe by having them do something at the end of the video to demonstrate this.

For learning events, as part of your earliest preparation, ask senior leaders or relevant experts to provide a welcoming video clip – either as part of the joining instructions or to kick-start the actual session. This not only demonstrates their commitment to the event: our experience shows it increases interest and improves outcomes – even when the individual can't make the virtual event.

Whatever medium you choose, the important thing is *anything* you send to participants in advance can save time and increase engagement, helping you maximise the time you have together in the virtual classroom. The number one barrier to success of any virtual event is participants not being prepared.

RECORDING SESSIONS

Virtual events are easy to share with those who didn't attend. But, consider whether you need to record the session and, if so, inform participants it is being recorded and how it will be used afterwards. If there are any concerns, engage *briefly* with participants about that and, if necessary, agree to discuss it later.

You also need to decide how much you are going to record. For example, will breakout rooms be private?

It is really important for people to understand all the parameters *in advance*. So you need to get into the details. Will the recorded session sent out be audio-only or video, for example? Participants might not want a video recording of themselves on a webinar sent out to a bunch of people they don't know post-event – consent is essential, otherwise they might hold back in their participation. Make sure you communicate these details to everyone concerned. Without making these confidentiality-related decisions clear, there can be a real barrier to participants learning, sharing, being open and giving opinions.

THE EVENT ITSELF

This section looks at the organisation of a session.

STAGGERING START TIMES

It's wise to think about whether your event needs everyone there for the duration, or whether you can stagger start times. Particularly when facilitating meetings, more is not necessarily better. People are grateful for more free time. It's great to be able to say beforehand: 'We don't need David, Raj and Eve for the whole meeting. In terms of segments, it'll be 40 minutes for the first and for that we'll only need Megan, Nick and Olga. The rest of you, it'd be great if you could arrive at 10:45, when we'll summarise what we've agreed, and then move on from there.'

This kind of forward thinking is almost always appreciated: particularly if you summarise and bring them up to speed accurately upon their return. Busy attendees will also thank you for making your 60-minute meeting a maximum of 45–50 minutes.

THE WAITING ROOM

Many video-conferencing platforms have a waiting room, or equivalent. This is the screen you see before the meeting actually starts and the host admits everyone. Some people will turn up to your event early – and this could be very early if you are working across time zones, or people don't factor in daylight saving changes and arrive an hour early.

This is an opportunity to welcome people, to remind them of prerequisites, or to otherwise set the scene. You can generally customise this experience and may be able to add images. This will help people to feel welcome, and overcome their first anxiety: are they in the right place.

You can also use this space to let participants know when the session starts, and if there are delays.

THE BIT WHERE PEOPLE ARE COMING INTO THE ROOM

Think about how you can build rapport while you wait for the session to start properly. In face-to-face interactions people arrive and there follow all those usual acknowledgements – even rituals – such as handshakes and chit-chat on seven subjects: the weather; where people live; families or mutual acquaintances; travel to the venue; holidays; their work, or the meeting itself.

How can you replicate this experience? It's a necessary part of the group learning experience as people feel their way into the mood of the room and the characters they will be interacting with.

If you welcome each attendee by name and encourage them to talk on the above subjects they're familiar with, it helps them to assimilate into the virtual room.

It can feel excluding if people chat away familiarly and you don't know anyone. It's bad enough in a physical environment, but more daunting online.

You can encourage people to use the chat facility privately if they want to have a side conversation, or if they know each other.

You might also put people into virtual breakout rooms where they can get to know each other before the programme starts. If you have scheduled your first breakout early in your session, this will help and it's a good idea to extend the first session by a couple of minutes to allow people to get to know each other and settle in.

THE CRUCIAL OPENING

People love variety and don't want to experience the same old, same old. This maxim is true for the physical world and crucial in the virtual world, where a screen and distance separate participants. Proactively plan your introduction to the session to ensure that you keep them curious and constantly learning from the first minute to the last.

The first ten minutes of any session are crucial. This is where you build initial trust and understanding, both in yourself as the facilitator *and* in the technology.

CREATE A SAFE PLACE TO LEARN

You need to create an atmosphere and safe environment for learning and decision-making where people want to join in and remain involved.

Some things you might want to think about to create such an atmosphere:

- What can you see in their background that you can connect with?
- What do they seem to care about?
- What might be worrying them?
- Will their technology work?
- Will they be interrupted?
- Will they see themselves on video?
- How will they sound?

CONVERSATIONS AND RELATIONSHIPS

Your second immediate goal is setting the foundations for guiding the conversations to build relationships with the goal of harnessing the collective energy of participants to develop skills, knowledge and behaviours, and to maximise their experience.

The best learning often occurs when participants are in their discomfort zones, where they feel stretched, but to enable them to do this they have to first feel the environment is right.

If you get this right you will create a discovery learning environment, where participants:

- learn from each other and their experiences.
- understand what is meaningful for them.

- receive feedback from the facilitator and their peer group that is real and genuine.

There is often more anxiety for participants online than at physical events. Your greeting can help to dispel this apprehension.

Early conversations help to establish connections and build credibility. But there's still the tech side to consider. Ask explicitly:

- Are you hearing me well?
- Can you see me properly?
- Is the connection OK?
- Is anything not working for you?

If you are struggling to hear someone, tell them early in the conversation. If multiple people are on the call, you could send a private message in the chat to let them know they're not connected.

SETTING EXPECTATIONS

Once you've got small talk out the way and you've made people feel comfortable with the virtual environment they're in, you need to clearly set expectations for the session, namely:

- what you're going to be doing
- your desired outcomes
- what the participants can expect from you
- what you expect from them

You want a contribution from each participant as early as possible, either verbally or in the chat box. If this doesn't happen, they are less likely to actively contribute later. Tell them things like: 'I'd love to hear from each of you', 'Everyone's contribution matters' and 'The more you contribute the richer this time will be.' The aim is to get some response from everyone within the first few minutes.

You won't get another chance as good as this to win your participants over. Your interaction, confidence, clarity, direction and energy will give them certainty, and pave the way for the best possible outcomes.

SETTING GROUND RULES

There are practical considerations, and you also need to set the tone for what acceptable and unacceptable behaviour looks like. There are key things to think about:

PERSONAL COMFORT

Make it clear that it is OK for people to stand up, stretch, move around and do whatever they have to in order to be comfortable and fully present. If you don't, it may be distracting when someone does this. It's important to remember that some attendees may have physical restrictions, disabilities or specific needs. In fact, for most people, asking them to stand and stretch in the middle of a session can be subtly revitalising. Make sure they're on board with this type of request. Some people will feel silly doing it, and shouldn't be forced to comply.

Simply asking for a thumbs-up does wonders for energy levels – it's too easy for people to drift into their own thoughts online. There's a whole section earlier that covers engagement tips you can review for more ideas.

HOW TO JOIN THE CONVERSATION

Highlight how to get your attention – whether it's letting you know they've got something to say or to answer a question. The last thing you want is say is: 'Sorry, Will, but could you please signal before you ask a question?' as that can feel like a snub and Will might decide not to contribute for the next half-hour, if ever. Give them a choice of three options:

- raising their physical hand
- raising their electronic hand
- contacting you in the chat function

Get everyone onto gallery or side-by-side view so you can see everyone, and then get them to physically raise their hand to the screen. Do the same thing with electronic hands. We also recommend that you ask everyone to use gallery view too, so they can see their colleagues.

TIMINGS

Be crystal-clear about timings. Let everyone know when the breaks will happen, how long they'll have, and what to do if they have to leave the session early. 'We're going to have a break at 11:00 for 15 minutes' or 'At noon, I've scheduled a break for an hour' or 'Should you need to leave any session early, please remember to put a note in the chat so we know you are OK. Thanks!'

EXPLAIN THE TOOLS YOU WILL USE

Explain any tools you are using *just prior to the time they'll need to use them.* If anyone's unfamiliar with the system, or if you're using tools like the whiteboard, explain it, and make sure that you do a quick practice-run before they attempt to use it for real. This dry run is also helpful as people, especially creatives, tend to get energised the first time they draw or stamp on a slide or whiteboard and things can get out of hand quickly. It's great to get this out of their system before they use it for real.

USE OF THE MUTE FUNCTION

The larger the group the more important it is to get people to stay on mute unless specifically invited to come off mute and contribute.

Open plan offices, affectionate pets and playful children, etc can be distracting background noises for everyone.

USE OF CHAT FUNCTION

It's also wise to highlight that you might not have time to get to answer each individual contribution in the chat. This is why it's great to work in a team. The larger the group the more important it is to have more than one person on hand to answer questions, or at least note them all down so they get a response either in the meeting or afterwards.

In larger groups, do your best to direct questions and comments to the chat. Thirty people interrupting your flow every few minutes will seriously impact everyone's learning experience.

While it's crucial to get names right, how they're pronounced and spelled, you don't need to be so pedantic about other grammar and language. Make sure everyone knows that typos are allowed, every question is welcomed and that different perspectives are valued.

GALLERY VIEW

It's highly advisable to ask participants to use gallery view so they can see the whole meeting.

Even if you're in a large group, it's still worth asking that people put their screen onto gallery view, at least briefly. It's a great feeling to be able to say: 'So, we've got seventy people on the call, but just one agenda!' etc.

ACCEPTABLE LANGUAGE & MUTUAL RESPECT

Bad language and swearing can be a sensitive area in the workplace and in training environments. In some places it might be considered abnormal not to swear, and in others it's an absolute *faux pas*. In a face-to-face environment tempers can fray and voices can be raised. People may respond to bad language and raised voices differently, and cues of unease are easier to read in a physical room. Managing these types of situations is something most facilitators have dealt with and we take it for granted that facilitators are keen and able to manage this sensitively.

What makes it trickier to handle online are the reduction in non-verbal communication and the ability of people to switch off – literally. Calming gestures and expressions can be missed by the protagonists and if someone wants to walk out and not come back, it's much easier to do online.

In most professional settings this is unlikely to be an issue, but for educators working with younger or more challenging participants, acceptable behaviour needs to be addressed early in the process.

WELCOME-BACK RITUAL

If you are going to have breakout rooms, breaks or other points where people will disperse for a set time, you might want to use a welcome-back routine. Playing the same piece of music, for example, can act as a gentle cue for everyone to return, and signal how long they have.

ASK FOR CLARIFICATION

Ask if there is anything you've forgotten or anything that someone would like to add or clarify.

DISPLAY NAMES

Names matter. If your name shows up automatically as Edward and you prefer to be called Ed, it matters. For some, it might be a company name that comes up. If you say: 'Please check your name and see if it's how you prefer to be known', don't be surprised if around 50% of people immediately change it. This shows that it's not only worth asking, but it also gives participants choice and a feeling of equal status.

Or, you can shake it up and ask them to name themselves after their favourite superhero, their pet's name, or their favourite character from the Netflix series they're currently binge-watching.

This activity not only familiarises them with the technology but also gives them an activity to engage in early in the meeting. More crucially, it sets up the mindset of this being a relaxed and safe environment. At the same time, it permits you to see who hasn't found the button yet and to gently support them: 'I notice, Krush and Laura, that you haven't changed your names yet?'

Note that group size has an impact here. You can probably get 20 people to change their names but unlikely for 100 – not only because the level of interaction you're going to have with them is reduced, but also because being able to support people who don't know how to change their names would be a logistical nightmare.

If you aren't sure how to pronounce someone's name, ask them to come off mute and say their name to ensure you get it right. Participants appreciate that and they'll know that you really want to get it right for them. You'll want them to end the session feeling they have been seen and heard, and were able to think and learn in a safe and enjoyable environment. Getting names right is an important step in making this happen.

ICEBREAKERS

Icebreakers are a natural evolution of early engagement conversations. They enable people to get to know you and each other – and to see you as a real person. You have to work a bit at this: it's not like in a physical space, where you'll probably be observed walking down the corridor, talking, getting a drink and chatting about your family before you even enter the room.

A good icebreaker activity is to get people to write who they are, where they are and what they do into the chat box. How the facilitator comments on what people put into the chat is really important. 'Beverley, I notice you mention having made great progress this week. That's fantastic – please come off mute and tell us about it!'

This type of interactivity makes people feel acknowledged as people rather than just anonymous chat commentators.

Ask participants at the start to type into the chat box to ensure they all know where it is and how it works. It could be something trivial: what they had for breakfast. It could be one of the seven opening gambits or something topical to the day's news.

Another option: relate a short personal anecdote of your own (maximum of two minutes) or ask them to write down three things people probably don't know about them – and share your own.

Depending on where they are and how well they know each other, asking: 'What's the temperature like where you are?' or 'What's the last programme you watched?' allows them to build connections. You could also ask them to pick up something around them and show it to the group, show-and-tell style. Ideally, it's something the group wouldn't expect to see on their desk (and hope it's fit for public consumption!).

You're aiming for light-hearted information that builds mutual understanding and allows people to move towards respecting, liking and trusting each other.

If all participants already know each other you can go deeper. Questions like: 'What's the most challenging thing happening in your world at the moment – in work or outside of it?' work well. People are often happy to share. For example, one of our recent participants said: "I p's"This was helpful on a several levels. People got the message and understood his situation. They were likely to feel compassion and empathy rather than questioning his commitment if he had to leave. When he did indeed have to briefly leave, instead of thinking: 'Probably off to check his emails!' the other team members clearly felt compassion, support and understanding – a far more productive environment for working and learning.

BEING INCLUSIVE AND MAKING COMPROMISES

It's important to create an inclusive environment, where people feel they have choices. We can encourage participants to put their cameras on, but if someone doesn't want to put theirs on, we need to respect that. With luck, they might be persuaded to do so in the breakout rooms as this is often a compromise people are willing to make.

In face-to-face training someone might leave their coat on, and only take it off when they feel they are staying. Virtually, there are similar ways in which people will consciously, or subconsciously, need to settle in. People have preferred ways of working and some are yet to find their feet in this brave new virtual world.

Find out early on if there's any resistance and adapt your style accordingly. Never force participants into trying anything that they are firmly resistant to. You may be able to influence them to try new things later. There is a fine line between challenging attendees to extend themselves, and unnecessarily or prematurely pressuring them into uncomfortable territory.

You will need to be comfortable with silence because when you ask a question online the answer isn't always immediate. There are lots of reasons for this. People may be struggling to get off mute, or feeling reflective, or just wish to pause before speaking to a screen.

If people are dialling in (on a phone without video), it's a good idea to ask them to say their name before they speak as this will really help others to focus on the content rather than thinking, 'Hmm, who's that? Do I know them?' This also enables the people on the phone to feel 'seen' psychologically, if not on screen. You might sometimes have to remind people to be mindful about giving a speaker time to pause before rushing in and speaking over them.

DELIVERING YOUR CONTENT

Now you can start to deliver your content, according to your course design. If you're an experienced facilitator, this is where you are likely to be most comfortable. Now you're in the flow of the content itself, it can be easy to forget the differences in virtual delivery. This is the time to be most wary – when you're delivering on auto-pilot and in the zone. This is the time to remember to keep checking in with participants and ensuring that they are participating as fully as possible.

For some, this might be the most frustrating part of facilitation as there is often a desire to crack on with the content as it can feel as though things are going well. In fact, some participants have switched off and they will be lost until rescued.

SIGNPOSTING AND SUMMARISING

As you progress through your content you need to let everyone know where you all are. This may sound basic, but it's essential. 'We've covered the planning and language section of the programme, so we'll now move on to delivery.'

This is because participants lose track more easily in the virtual world, due to the bite-sized nature of the things they're doing, isolation and susceptibility to distraction.

Announce polls, breakout rooms and video clips before they begin, to prepare participants. It can be useful to narrate your actions as you prepare certain materials, to make your session feel like the sort of informal conversation that builds trust.

These signposts and summaries need to be planned once you're clear how you're going to link topics and sections together (a story, a visual reminder like a slide, a verbal summary, etc).

In big events, being able to summarise large amounts of information is an important skill.

A RUNNING COMMENTARY

Giving an overview of where you are in your own mind is an important skill in the virtual environment. 'I'm just about to launch the poll' or 'I can see that half of you have voted; we're just waiting for five people to complete their voting. There are thirty seconds left in which to have your say!'

A commentary of what's happening also helps people to understand where they are, and avoids long, uncomfortable silences. 'I'm just going to go back and download a new document for us to review. While I'm doing that, can you please write into the chat the most concerning issue for you with the current outline.'

WHAT IF YOU GET THINGS WRONG?

A useful tactic is to call yourself out when you make a mistake. 'I literally *cannot* believe I just did that; so sorry, I'll just rewind and start again.' It's better to get everyone to mentally reset than to fumble along in the wrong direction trying to wing it.

It also says that mistakes are allowed. Sometimes we all need to know that.

If you're having a conversation it needs to remain a conversation, even when you make a mistake. This builds trust and shows that you're comfortable and confident in yourself and in what you're doing.

GOING OFF-TOPIC

Someone brings up a subject not on the agenda. Then someone else says: 'We haven't got time.' Then a third person says: 'True, but we don't generally have a whole lot of time together and this seems really important to me.' This kind of issue can become both messy and time-consuming – but it might also be really important.

If this happens, you need to return to the agenda and remind people why they are there – and why it's important. This should get things back on track.

But, if you find this causing a genuine blockage, you can launch an impromptu poll: to stick with the original plan or to change direction. Voting isn't generally a good way to make team decisions, but sometimes it's a fast way to unblock a way forward.

Another option is to put all the perspectives onto the whiteboard and then make the decision.

If the issue isn't discussed, but is clearly important, it's crucial that it does get time, even if not here and now. If it's important enough it might warrant a dedicated session at another time.

ENDING THE SESSION

The end of an online session can feel very abrupt. As facilitators, we need to replicate the equivalent of saying 'Goodbye, have a great weekend and drive home safely.' If you don't manage the introduction and exit from the session in a human way, it subtly impacts on participants' experiences.

At the same time, it's not a great idea to drag it out; in the virtual world people really hate to overrun the agreed time unless you've decided at the outset that you might have to (and even then you need to be aware of resistant body language).

A solid way of wrapping up – and giving a sense of achievement and closure to the session – is to create a call to action. This could be:

- the next steps to be taken
- the next meeting time to be decided
- a quick review of how everyone is feeling
- summarise lessons learned
- ask participants to summarise how they feel in the chat
- ask for a review of the session

You should acknowledge comments in the chat you didn't get to.

In larger groups, you will probably have to acknowledge that you didn't get to hear from every member of the group.

You should also thank everyone involved for their contribution and single out any participants who have done something noteworthy. A nice option at the end of a session is to ask participants to make this peer acknowledgement in the chat for who has helped them or contributed to their thinking, and how. There's nothing like leaving a session with a warm glow of appreciation.

If there's a follow-up meeting it can be useful to end with a taster of what's to come. 'Next session we're exploring the three critical tools you need in order to influence key decision makers. Looking forward to seeing you all on Thursday!'

What is essential is to have time scheduled for whatever activity you intend to have at the end. It's unsatisfactory to rush through this at speed because you only allowed two minutes to wrap it up.

EXAMPLE SCHEDULE

There are many possible formats for online events. From single sessions of 60–90 minutes to 12-month courses. What follows is a sample of a single session, which can provide a template for multiple sessions.

When you run multiple sessions with the same people you can cut down on the explanation of tech, chat, etc, but don't be tempted to just jump straight into content. You still need to allow people time to figuratively take their coats off and re-connect with fellow attendees.

For your own planning and execution we suggest you create a template plan and then customise it according to the overall objectives, number of sessions, number of participants, etc.

This sample plan is for a single session of a course of six sessions as a taste of how you might structure and prepare your course schedules. You will, no doubt, have session plans and teaching aids already, so it may be possible to simply adapt and change what you already have. Remember, however, that whatever you have prepared for face-to-face events will need to be greatly reduced for online delivery.

A PLAN FOR A SINGLE SESSION

This isn't the blueprint for every session – it's an example, and an extract at that. The full plan we use is in landscape format and contains more notes: basically, anything that can help with delivery and to ensure we cover our essential content. Some of the timings may prove useful, but every facilitator will design their own format that they find comfortable and effective. Once you have a plan that works, rinse and repeat, but remember to reflect and, perhaps, refresh and revise.

Course: [Course Title]

Session: [Session Title]

Duration: 90 minutes – no breaks

Session number: 3 of 6

Location/platform: Virtual / *Platform X*

Target audience: [Audience]

No. of attendees: 16

Presentation team:

- AB (primary facilitator)
- CD (co-presenter / tech support)

Module Description:

This session gives you time personally and in small groups to stop and reflect about the current global situation and what it all means to you as individuals, family, team members and leaders.

Purpose: To give participants some time to stop and think and reflect together.

Objectives:

During the event, participants will:

- [Learning point 1]
- [Learning point 2]
- [Learning point 3]

Pre-event:

- Send link to recorded video intro from facilitators, seek a response to the video (see outline below)
- Quick overview of the sessions
- Email pre-course materials
- Tech – email standard instruction sheet on setting up *Platform X*

Session timings:

-30:00 to -05:00 | KM & CD

- Check tech and review running order and roles

-05:00 to 00:00 | CD

- Housekeeping slide ready for entry
- Early entrants can be allocated to breakout rooms to get acquainted

00:00 to 10:00 | Both

- Introductions to AB & CD (AB)
- Brief intros for attendees (AB)
- Tech check (CD)
- Prompt everyone to use gallery view (CD)
- Purpose of the session (AB)
- Personal comfort – stretching, hydration, etc (AB)

11:00 to 20:00 | Q&A / AB

- Topic 1
- Questions slide on screen and ask participants to put 3 words each in chat
- Ask for volunteers to share experience (CD)

21:00 to 40:00 | Breakout rooms / CD

- Topic 2
- Three people in each room – delegate to feed back
- Discussion questions on screen
- Half-way message and 1 minute to go
- 7 minutes for breakout, then 11 minutes for feedback and discussion

41:00 to 50:00 | Video / AB

- Topic 3
- Topic 3 slide
- Topic 3 video (1:45 running time)
- Tell story and discuss key themes
- Request comments in chat
- Send Topic 3 resources at the end of the session

51:00 to 70:00 | Breakout rooms / AB

- Topic 4
- Topic 4 slide
- Same groups as before
- Half-way message and 1 minute to go (CD)
- 7 minutes for breakout, then 11 minutes for feedback and discussion

71:00 to 85:00 | Breakout rooms / AB

- Topic 5
- Topic 5 slide
- Same groups as before
- Half-way message and 1 minute to go (CD)
- 6 minutes for breakout, then 9 minutes for feedback and discussion

86:00 to 90:00 | KM

- Close
- Thanks for attention, involvement and mention contributions
- Reminder for next session date and time
- Summarise agreed learnings

Post-session:

- Send resources and slides (CD)
- Post-session review (both)
- Check with client for feedback (AB)
- Possible re-design for next session (both)

VIDEO RECORDING FROM FACILITATORS

Here's a suggestion for a script for a pre-event video invitation. Adapt it to your own needs: add or subtract as you see fit.

1. We look forward to seeing you on our call on [DATE] at [LOCAL TIME]. We would encourage you to join the session 15 minutes early to make sure the technology is working OK.
2. The purpose of this time together is to give you some time to stop and think.
3. So, before the session we ask you to have a think about your feelings and thoughts of the last eight weeks... and indeed those of others.
4. We recognise this time may not have been easy for you, and so this session remains entirely confidential. We will not be recording or capturing anything other than your feedback at the end, so we encourage you to share as much as you can to both learn and develop your ideas, while also seeking to keep the conversation emotionally safe.
5. We entirely respect that many of you will be at home or in an open-plan office and there may be other distractions, although we ask that you try and plan for this and set yourself up in a quiet environment where possible.
6. Headphones may improve your experience.
7. Check in advance your wi-fi internet connection is stable and the link is working. We have emailed a technology setup guide for *Platform X*, which we will be using.
8. Use a laptop/desktop where possible and try to avoid using a phone, otherwise you may be unable to fully participate in the interactive exercises.
9. We look forward to seeing you [DATE AND LOCAL TIME].

POST-EVENT

Your normal methods for post-course evaluation may need adaptation in the virtual setting. That's not to say you have to start from scratch.

It's easy to assume that every participant is set up with the ideal home office, but this would be false. Anything that requires a signature should be made available to complete online wherever possible. Not everyone has mastered or has access to printers, scanners, email, or a mobile phone which might do all of this.

You can still send out questionnaires, but consider moving these to online versions instead. It can be frustrating to receive a Word document that changes its format on opening, or a PDF that doesn't behave properly, or not be able to check the boxes or mark answers. It's easier for the recipient to use online forms where the technology ensures consistent presentation, and they only need a web browser to complete it. There are plenty of free and paid solutions to choose from; just search for 'online surveys' for suggestions. You may have software in use that includes this feature already.

One-to-one conversations or meetings you might have had in person will now have to be scheduled online or over the phone. Impromptu group discussions will require online facilitation and may lose some of their spontaneity.

Your existing testing and evaluation of the efficacy of your training will still work, but consider the impact from the learner's perspective. If they left your session with unasked or unanswered questions, they require a mechanism to get resolution, and whatever method you choose, it needs to be communicated to them, and available in a user-friendly format.

Disengagement after the session may not always be an issue, but any ongoing programme requiring follow-up will have to take in consideration the dynamics at play of online learning.

CONNECT WITH KEVIN

I hope this book helps you in your transition to blending face-to-face and online facilitation. There will be challenges along the way, and things won't always run smoothly. There will also be successes and highs. If you would like to share your experiences or ask questions please connect with me on LinkedIn and we can grow together.

I wish you well on your journey.

www.linkedin.com/in/KevinMcAlpin-coach